THE
Vegetable
Garden Planner

A Crop-by-Crop Guide
for Planning and Tracking Your Garden Bounty Each Year,
from Seed Starting to Harvest

LYNN BYCZYNSKI

Storey Publishing

The mission of Storey Publishing is to serve our customers by publishing practical information that encourages personal independence in harmony with the environment.

Edited by Carleen Madigan
Art direction and book design by Bredna Lago
Text production by Jennifer Jepson Smith

Cover and interior illustration credits appear on page 203

Storey Publishing
210 MASS MoCA Way
North Adams, MA 01247
storey.com

Storey Publishing, LLC is an imprint of Workman Publishing Co., Inc., a subsidiary of Hachette Book Group, Inc., 1290 Avenue of the Americas, New York, NY 10104

ISBN: 978-1-63586-658-2 (paperback)

Printed in China by Imago
10 9 8 7 6 5 4 3 2 1

Contents

HOW TO USE THIS PLANNER

Welcome to a new approach to garden planning and record keeping! Rather than being arranged chronologically, as virtually every gardening notebook until now has been, this journal is arranged by the type of crop. Each crop is introduced with basic advice for getting it off to a good start, followed by a page where you can record your experiences with that crop. When you've filled that page, you can continue your notes in the additional record-keeping pages toward the back of the book. Add notes year after year, to create what will become a customized planner for your garden.

The advantage of this format is that you won't need to go through a stack of previous years' notebooks to remember what you planted, where you bought it, and how well it did. Instead, you can keep all those records in one place for a quick review at the start of each season. As experienced gardeners know, keeping track of your garden is essential to improving it. If you are diligent about writing down everything you do, you can easily duplicate successes and avoid failures.

Keys to Success

Some things about gardening are the same wherever you grow, such as proper soil preparation and fertility, watering, and weed control. In my experience, though, once you've mastered these practices, the two most important factors to successful gardening are variety selection and scheduling.

Choosing the Best Variety

For every vegetable you choose to grow, you will find that multiple—in some cases, literally hundreds—of varieties are available to you, ranging from centuries-old heirlooms to this year's newest hybrids. Reading seed catalogs in winter and ordering new-to-you varieties are part of a long gardening tradition. But not every variety of a vegetable will be equally successful in your garden. Varieties vary in productivity, disease resistance, cold and heat tolerance, flavor, and many other factors. Your job is to find those that do best in your particular conditions and that taste best to you. As you explore new varieties, keeping records is essential. I always think I will never forget anything about my garden, but I have learned not to trust my memory completely—a written record is much more reliable. And if you garden with a partner, a journal will head off future disagreements.

Getting the Timing Right

Timing can be just as important as variety selection. You have to work around the natural limitations of the vegetables, such as whether they require cool or warm temperatures plus their days to maturity. Your own climate will dictate which vegetables you can grow and when you can grow them. For example, if your frost-free season is only 90 days, it's pointless to grow a tomato that takes 85 days to mature. Or if the weather turns from occasional late freezes to blazing

heat practically overnight in spring (that's my climate), it will be hard to get a spring crop of radicchio, which bolts if it's too cold or too warm. By recording your planting dates and the results, you can refine your scheduling over the years. You may even be able to juggle planting dates to avoid common insect and disease problems.

Making the Most of Your Journal

The more information you record in this journal, the more helpful it will become year after year. Write small and neatly so you can use the book for many years. Start each entry with the full date, and make a note of these facts:

- Variety and where you bought the seeds or plants
- Dates of seeding and transplanting
- Dates of other cultivation practices such as trellising, spraying, etc.
- Notes on weather anomalies such as a freak late frost or early heat spell
- Date of first harvest and duration of harvest
- Comments on flavor and yield
- Advice to yourself on how to do better next year

For example, let's say you were unimpressed with your onions last year but you remember having a great onion crop a few years ago. If you have maintained this journal, you can turn to the section on onions and scan back through multiple years of notes. Look for enthusiastic comments you wrote about your onions. Figure out if your planting dates or weather conditions were different from those in the good year. Replicate your successful planting, and you are more likely to be happy this year.

The front of the journal contains useful tables for quick reference. It also contains prompts for you to write down information you would otherwise have to look up every year, such as your first and last frost dates and the approximate dates for starting seeds in your climate. You can sketch plant placement in the garden on special pages (a big help in planning crop rotations). And in the back of the book, you'll find pages where you can create your own records for crops that aren't specifically mentioned.

Although a great deal about gardening is the same for every gardener in every location, your garden is actually unique. Learning what works for you—and then replicating that process in future years—is the best way to a successful garden. In gardening, experience truly is the best teacher.

—LYNN BYCZYNSKI

MY
Garden Basics

Look up and record the information you will need
every year to schedule your plantings.

Frost Dates

Deciding when to plant in the spring and when to rush out and toss row covers over your crops in the fall can seem like a gamble. The last frost in spring and the first frost in fall don't happen predictably on the same days every year. Nature also doesn't turn on a dime, with heavy frosts up until a certain date, then no frosts at all until the fall. The change in weather happens gradually, with decreasing chances of frost as the spring progresses.

Because of that, it's up to you to decide when is the right time to plant, based on what types of crops you're growing (see page 10) and how much risk you want to take. It's helpful to learn the frost dates for your area and use them as guidelines for when to plant in spring and when to protect plants in fall. Even with these average dates at hand, it's a good idea to check the two-week forecast regularly, to home in on specific dates when freezing temperatures may occur.

Frost Categories and Likelihood

Frosts are categorized by severity. Gardeners need to distinguish between levels of frost, because certain annual crops are killed with less frost than others are.

A light frost is 32°F/0°C. This will damage tender warm-weather plants such as tomatoes and basil, but most cold-weather plants such as broccoli and lettuce will be fine.

A heavy frost is 28°F/−2°C. This will damage all but the most cold-tolerant plants.

A severe frost is 24°F/−4°C or below. This will kill almost all annual crops.

Be aware that a frost can occur whenever the temperature drops below 36°F/2°C, depending on other conditions; for example, frosts are more likely to occur on a clear night with no wind. The National Weather Service will issue a warning when conditions are right for frost over a wide area, but you may find your garden is a microclimate where frost occurs sooner or later than the surrounding area. (Also note that, although gardeners have traditionally referred to "frost-free dates," the National Weather Service now uses the term "freeze dates.")

Find Your Average Frost Dates

In addition to categorizing frost temperatures by level of severity, agencies like the National Weather Service give percentages for the likelihood a certain level of frost will happen on certain dates. Many gardeners use the date after which there is a 50 percent likelihood of 32°F/0°C temperatures as their "last frost date" for spring or "first frost date" for fall. These are the dates we'll be using throughout the book to schedule seed starting, and we'll refer to them as the "average date of final spring frost" and the "average date of first fall frost."

You can find the frost date information for your garden by entering your zip code in the app found at garden.org/apps /frost-dates. The data are based on historic temperatures for a National Weather Service station near your location. Write down your average frost dates. You'll refer to these often.

My Average Frost Dates

Average Date of Final Spring Frost	
Average Date of First Fall Frost	

My Actual Frost Date Records

Use this table to record your actual frost dates each year.

Year	Final Frost in Spring	First Frost in Fall

Frost Tolerance of Crops

Frost tolerance in the garden varies according to many factors, including cultivar, plant maturity and health, and soil moisture. Plants that originated in northern climates are more likely to withstand frost, whereas those from tropical climates will be killed. Mature plants are more frost-tolerant than young plants. In spring, young plants that have been hardened off outside will tolerate frost better than those that have come straight from indoors. In fall, plants grown in gradually decreasing temperatures can withstand more cold than those exposed to a sudden cold snap. Although there are no hard-and-fast rules about cold tolerance, some generalizations can be made:

Plants that cannot tolerate any frost: basil, beans, corn, cucumbers, eggplant, melons, okra, peppers, potatoes, summer and winter squash, tomatoes

Plants that can tolerate a light frost (29 to 32°F/–2 to 0°C): beets, broccoli, cauliflower, cabbage, celery, chard, leeks, lettuce, mustard, onions, parsley, peas, sweet potatoes

Plants that can tolerate a hard frost (28°F/–2°C and below; may even survive winter with protection): arugula, beets, Brussels sprouts, carrots, chicory, collards, kale, kohlrabi, mâche, parsnips, radishes, spinach, turnips

Day Length

Your growing season is not completely dependent on temperature; day length matters, too. Plants don't grow well with fewer than 10 hours of daylight. You can find a day-length calculator for your location at timeanddate.com/sun.

The dates when I have more than 10 hours of daylight:

_____

USDA Zone

The USDA Plant Hardiness Zone Map is not particularly relevant to vegetable gardening because it pertains to winter low temperatures. However, it's good to know your zone to determine which perennials will survive your usual winter.

I'm in USDA Zone _____

Succession Planting

Many crops can be planted several times in spring to spread out the harvest over a longer period. The recommended length of time between succession plantings is based on how long each planting will produce, and how long the vegetables can be stored without losing quality. Succession planting only works as long as the weather is conducive to growing that type of crop.

Plant every 2 weeks: arugula, bush beans, beets, broccoli, cauliflower, corn, kale, kohlrabi, lettuce, muskmelons, green onions, greens, radishes, spinach, tomatoes, turnips

Plant every 3 weeks: cabbage, carrots

Plant every 4–5 weeks: cucumbers, summer squash

Plant every 8 weeks: eggplants

Getting Advice

The best place to seek guidance to gardening problems is from your local Cooperative Extension Service. It provides homeowners with solid information about gardening in your location. You will find gardening guides on most state Extension websites, and many have printed publications in their offices. Extension offices will do a soil test for a small fee. Many state land-grant universities conduct variety trials of garden crops, and Extension agents disseminate the results to help gardeners choose the varieties most likely to succeed in their area. Extension agents also can help diagnose disease and pest problems. The Extension Service oversees the state Master Gardener program, which trains volunteers in the art and science of gardening in exchange for community work.

Search online for "Cooperative Extension" plus your county and state names, and record the contact information for your local office here.

Website: _____

Email: _____

Phone: _____

Horticulture or home gardening agent: _____

_____

As you do garden research online, you are likely to find certain websites that appeal to you for one reason or another. Keep a list here of sites you want to visit in the future.

Favorite gardening websites:_____

_____

_____

_____

_____

Indoor Seed-Starting Schedule—Spring

Weeks before Average Date of Final Spring Frost	My Dates*	Vegetables
10–12 weeks		Asparagus, artichoke, celery, celeriac, leeks, onions
8–10 weeks		Eggplant, peppers, tomatoes
6–7 weeks		Chicory, lettuce
4–5 weeks		Broccoli, cabbage, cauliflower, collards, kale, kohlrabi, okra, spinach, Swiss chard
3–4 weeks		Cucumbers, melons, pumpkins, squash

*Count back from your average date of final spring frost and record the approximate date to start seeds indoors.

Outdoor Direct-Seeding Schedule—Spring

Weeks Relative to Average Date of Final Spring Frost	My Dates*	Vegetables
3–4 weeks before		Arugula, carrots, lettuce (baby), peas, radishes, spinach, turnips
1–2 weeks before		Beet, chicory (leaf types), lettuce (head), parsley
On average date of final spring frost		Parsnips, perennial herbs
1 week after		Beans, corn
2 weeks after		Basil, cucumbers, pumpkins, squash

*Count back and forward from your average date of final spring frost and record the approximate date to plant seeds outside. Verify that no freezing temperatures are in the two-week forecast when planting warm-weather crops.

Starting Herbs from Seed

	Weeks before Average Date of Final Spring Frost*	My Dates	Days to Germination**
Anise	12		4–9
Basil	6–8		5–8
Borage	6–8		5–8
Catnip	6–8		5–8
Chives	12		14
Cilantro	6–8		7–10
Dill***	6–8		5–8
Fennel	6–8		7–10
Lavender***	15–18		14–21
Marjoram	8–10		5–8
Mint	10–12		14
Oregano	10–12		5–8
Parsley	10–12		14–21
Rosemary***	12–15		10–15
Sage	10–12		6–10
Summer savory***	8–10		12–15
Thyme***	12–15		5–8

*Weeks before Average Date of Final Spring Frost assumes you will plant herbs outside around the time of the final frost in spring.

**Days to Germination is based on a seed-starting temperature of 70 to 80°F (21 to 27°C). Cooler temperatures will mean longer time to germination.

***Varieties that require light to germinate. Do not cover the seeds with soil; use a thin scattering of vermiculite and keep misted until germination.

Fall Gardening

In areas with freezing winter weather, it's important to calculate the last date when you can start seeds and hope to get a crop before it's killed by freezing temperatures. The tables below show when to start transplants indoors or direct seed outdoors, so the plants have sufficient time to mature. They incorporate typical days to maturity for fall varieties plus a "fall factor" of 14 additional days to account for slower growth as the day length gets shorter. Frost dates are just averages, though, so keep an eye on the forecast and be prepared to protect your fall crops with row cover when temperatures threaten to dip to 32°F (0°C).

Indoor Seed-Starting Schedule—Fall

Weeks before Average Date of First Fall Frost	My Dates	Vegetables
16–18 weeks		Brussels sprouts, cabbage, celery, celeriac, fennel, kale, leeks, peas
12–13 weeks		Broccoli, cauliflower, chicory, collards
10 weeks		Chinese cabbage, endive, escarole, lettuce (head)

Outdoor Direct-Seeding Schedule—Fall

Weeks before Average Date of First Fall Frost	My Dates	Vegetables
12–13 weeks		Carrots, onions, peas, radishes (daikon), rutabaga
10–11 weeks		Beets, lettuce (leaf), kohlrabi, radishes (round), spinach, Swiss chard, turnips

Planning Your Garden Layout and Rotations

On page 16, list the vegetables and herbs you want to grow. For each type, list the number of plants or linear feet you think you can use. In the crop-by-crop section, look up the recommended spacing. Then sketch out your garden space to make sure you have room for everything you want to grow.

As you plan your garden, aim to rotate crops into a new space each year. In general, plants in the same family should be grown together and moved to a new spot the next year, because they tend to have similar nutrient requirements and be affected by the same insects and disease. If possible, try for a four-year rotation of every plant family.

Here is a list of plant families:

Carrot family: carrots, celery, parsley, parsnips

Goosefoot family: beets, chard, spinach

Gourd family: cucumbers, melons, watermelons, summer and winter squash, pumpkins

Mustard family: broccoli, Brussels sprouts, cabbages, cauliflower, collards, kale, kohlrabi, mustard greens, radishes, rutabagas, turnips

Nightshade family: eggplants, peppers, potatoes, tomatoes

Onion family: chives, garlic, leeks, onions, shallots

Bean family: beans and peas

Sunflower family: escarole, endive, lettuce, sunflowers

Seed Viability

Most vegetable seeds remain viable for years, as long as you keep them cool and dry. A good rule for seed storage is that the sum of temperature (in Fahrenheit) plus percent relative humidity should be no more than 100. For example, at 70°F (21°C), relative humidity should be no more than 30 percent. You can stay within this guideline by storing seeds in a cool place in an airtight plastic box or glass jar with a pouch of desiccant.

The table below shows the expected viability of seeds held at ideal conditions. If conditions were less than ideal, you may still have viable seeds.

If you're in doubt, viability is easy to test. Count out a specific number of seeds, say 10 to 20, and place them on a moistened paper towel or coffee filter. Put them in a sealable plastic bag and leave them in a warm, dark spot for the usual days to germination for that vegetable. Count the number of sprouts to determine the germination percentage. If it's below 50 percent, you may want to purchase new seeds, or you can plant more thickly than usual.

Expected Time Frame for Seed Viability*

Length of Time	Crop
5 years	Arugula, collard, cucumber, endive, muskmelon, radish
4 years	Beets, Brussels sprout, cabbage, cauliflower, chicory, eggplant, fennel, kale, mustard, pumpkin, rutabaga, squash, Swiss chard, tomato, turnip, watermelon
3 years	Asparagus, bean, broccoli, carrot, celeriac, celery, Chinese cabbage, kohlrabi, peas, spinach
2 years	Artichoke, cardoon, corn, leek, okra, pepper
1 year	Lettuce, onion, parsley, parsnip, salsify (1 year is a minimum, so test if you have a lot of leftover seed. Lettuce is particularly variable and may remain viable up to 6 years.)

*For vegetable seeds held in favorable conditions

Draw Your Garden Plan

Use this space to draw your garden plan, based on the number of crops you'd like to grow.

Draw Your Garden Plan, *continued*

MY
Crop Records

Keep careful records of the crops you grow each year, in order to improve your gardening skills, boost your harvest, and remember the details of individual varieties.

Artichoke and Cardoon

Cynara scolymus, C. cardunculus

Tricking Your Artichokes

Artichokes are perennial in Zones 7–11 and will produce flower buds in the second year; elsewhere, vernalization is required to "trick" them into acting like second-year plants. This involves putting 8-week-old plants outside in a protected area, where they will be exposed to temperatures of 45 to 50°F (7 to 10°C). After about 10 days of this cold treatment, the seedlings can be planted in the garden, ready to form buds as soon as the weather turns warm. Even using vernalization, artichokes are best grown in climates with cool summer weather. They do not do well in prolonged heat. Cardoons are somewhat more tolerant of heat than artichokes are, but drought will cause them to be tough and stringy.

Many people grow cardoons for their ornamental value as much as for their culinary use; the leaves are long, serrated, and silvery.

TP or DS: Transplant

Start seed: 10–12 weeks before average date of final spring frost

Seed depth: ¼"

Germination temperature: 70°F/21°C

Days to germination: 18–21

Growing temperature: 62°F/17°C

Transplant date: On average date of final spring frost

Spacing: 2–3' in row; 4–6' between rows

Ideal Seed-Starting Dates

Spring   /

Fall   /

Year/s

Varieties

....

Sources

....

Date	Notes on Seed Starting, Cultivation, Harvest, Yield, and Flavor

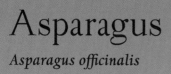

Asparagus

Asparagus officinalis

Growing from Seed

Asparagus can be grown from seed, but patience is required as germination can take several weeks and time to first harvest will be an extra year. However, heirloom varieties are often available only as seed, so don't be afraid to try them. Seedlings look like tiny asparagus spears when they first emerge. When plants are large enough to transplant, they can either be set out in the permanent asparagus bed or grown for a year in a nursery bed and transplanted the next spring. Pamper young plants with frequent weeding and irrigation.

Planting Crowns

Plant crowns in spring. Make a furrow 8 inches deep and place the crowns in a line, with buds 12 inches apart and roots all facing the same direction. Cover with 2 inches of soil. As spears grow, fill in the furrow. Mulch well to prevent weeds, and water regularly. Leave the fronds until they die back from cold, then cut to the ground. Harvest beginning the second spring after planting, but for only 2 weeks.

TP or DS: Transplant

Start seed: 12 weeks before average date of final spring frost

Seed depth: ½"

Germination temperature: 75 to 80°F/ 24 to 27°C

Days to germination: 21+ (up to 8 weeks)

Growing temperature: 70°F/21°C

Transplant date: On average date of last spring frost

Spacing: 8–12" in row; 3–6' between rows

Most people prefer to buy 1-year-old crowns when establishing these long-lived perennials.

Varieties

....

Sources

....

Date	Notes on Seed Starting, Cultivation, Harvest, Yield, and Flavor

Basil

Ocimum basilicum

**Purple varieties are
slower growing, so start them
a week earlier than green basil.**

TP or DS: Transplant

Start seed: 6–7 weeks before average date
of final spring frost

Seed depth: ¼"

Germination temperature: 70°F/20°C

Days to germination: 5–7

Growing temperature: 65°F/18°C

Transplant date: 1–2 weeks after average
date of last spring frost

Spacing: 12" in row; 2–3' between rows

Four Ways to Grow Basil

Basil plants are available in garden centers, but you really should try growing your own from seed because then you can grow them in several ways:

Let them flower. First, plant some individual plants and let them grow without pinching them, picking just leaves as you need them for the kitchen. The plants will eventually send up flower stems, which are pollinator magnets and fragrant cut flowers.

Pinch, root, and plant. The second method is to plant individual plants, and as they branch, pinch off small stems and place them in a glass of water. When they form roots, transplant them back into the garden.

Grow for an extended, tender harvest. The third method is the best way to get a long season of tender basil for cooking and pesto. It's also the best method if you've had disease problems with basil in the past. After the weather is warm, direct seed basil into the garden or a pot and cover lightly with fine soil. Keep moist until the seeds germinate. Allow the plants to get 4 to 6 inches tall, then begin to harvest them by pulling plants out by the roots. When you have a handful, trim off and discard the roots and place the stems in water like a bouquet. The small plants will be completely tender, and you can use them stems and all.

Bring indoors. Finally, if you have leftover seed in fall, sprinkle it in a pot that you can carry indoors when the weather gets cold. You can eat the seedlings as microgreens and garnish.

Ideal Seed-Starting Dates

Spring   /   Fall   /   **Year/s**

Varieties

....

Sources

....

Date	Notes on Seed Starting, Cultivation, Harvest, Yield, and Flavor

Beans

Phaseolus vulgaris

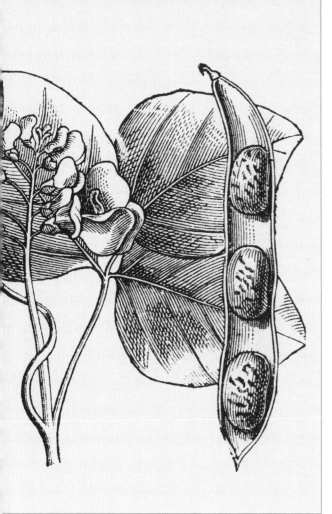

Bush or Pole?

The vegetables we call green beans, snap beans, or string beans are categorized by their growth habit.

Bush beans. These are determinate plants—they grow to maturity, bear over a condensed period of time, and then stop. For a continual harvest, succession plant them 2 weeks apart.

Pole beans. These keep growing and producing as long as the weather is warm. Pole beans require you to build a strong, tall trellis, but they are easier to pick, more productive per square foot of garden space, and are harvested over a long period. Pole beans should be planted just once.

Plan for heat. Both types of beans are best when the weather is warm but not too hot. When temperatures exceed 90°F (32°C) for a few days, bean flowers drop off without producing beans. If the heat persists, the plants will stop producing altogether. If your summers are that hot, plant bush beans as soon as the soil warms above 60°F (15°C). At the same time, plant other species of beans that are heat tolerant, such as lima beans and yard-long beans. They will take longer to bear but should carry you through the hottest part of summer. About 10 weeks before first frost in fall, plant bush beans again for a final crop.

TP or DS: Direct seed

Start seed: After average date of final spring frost

Seed depth: 1"

Germination temperature: >60°F/15°C daytime soil temp

Days to germination: 8–10

Growing temperature: 70 to 90°F/21 to 32°C

Transplant date: N/A

Spacing: Bush: 2" apart; pole: 3" apart. Space rows 3–4' apart.

Shelling beans are grown for their seeds, not their pods. They can be shelled and eaten fresh, or allowed to dry on the plant, then stored in glass jars for use in winter.

Ideal Seed-Starting Dates

Spring   /

Fall   /

Year/s

Varieties

....

Sources

....

Date	Notes on Seed Starting, Cultivation, Harvest, Yield, and Flavor

Beets

Beta vulgaris

Good Growing Tips

Sow every 2 weeks for a steady supply of roots and greens, which can be eaten like Swiss chard (which is actually the same species). To prevent misshapen roots, plant into a bed that is free of rocks and hard clumps of soil. Keep well weeded and mulched, because beets don't compete well with weeds. Beets can tolerate some shade. Don't plant them where potatoes, turnips, or carrots grew last year, to prevent the crop being spoiled by scab. Regular watering produces beets with smooth skin and great flavor.

Thin plants to prevent bolting. The most important thing to do for beets is to thin them to a final spacing of 4 to 6 inches. Plants that are not thinned are more likely to bolt without forming a beetroot. Seeds of most varieties are actually a cluster of fused embryos, so two or more seedlings may emerge from each seed, and some will need to be removed to provide adequate space between plants. Snip rather than pull the extras. Beet varieties that have only one embryo per seed will be described as "monogerm" and will require less thinning.

TP or DS: Direct seed

Start seed: 2–3 weeks before average date of final spring frost

Seed depth: ½"

Germination temperature: >45°F/7°C

Days to germination: 15

Growing temperature: 55 to 60°F/13 to 15°C

Transplant date: N/A

Spacing: 2" in row; 12" between rows

When you harvest beets, leave an inch of stem to prevent them from drying out in the refrigerator.

Varieties

....

Sources

....

Date	Notes on Seed Starting, Cultivation, Harvest, Yield, and Flavor

Broccoli and Cauliflower

Brassica oleracea var. *italica, B.o.* var. *botrytis*

Grow Brassicas Together

Broccoli and cauliflower (and all the brassicas, for that matter) are heavy feeders and should be grown in soil enriched with compost and organic fertilizer before planting. So many insects are attracted to brassicas that you might as well plant them all together, under row cover or insect netting held up by hoops.

Leave broccoli side shoots. Broccoli is tolerant of frost. It will produce a central head that should be harvested before the florets separate or yellow shows in the buds. Leave the plants, though, because broccoli will produce numerous side shoots that taste just as good or better than the main head.

Cauliflower needs special care. Cauliflower is fussier than broccoli. It requires cool temperatures but will not tolerate more than a light frost. Any weather stress can cause buttoning, in which the florets separate into clusters instead of making a smooth head. If that begins to happen, harvest the head, no matter what size it is.

The pure white heads of cauliflower are the result of blanching—a process that involves tying the outer leaves over the developing heads to prevent sunlight from reaching them. Some varieties, usually described as self-blanching, have big leaves that grow around the head naturally and don't require you to tie them. Nor do you need to tie up the leaves of purple, orange, or green varieties.

TP or DS: Transplant

Start seed: 6–8 weeks before average date of final spring frost

Seed depth: ¼"

Germination temperature: 70°F/21°C

Days to germination: 10

Growing temperature: 50 to 60°F/10 to 15°C

Transplant date: 2 weeks before average date of final spring frost

Spacing: 12–18" in row; 18–36" between rows

Ideal Seed-Starting Dates

Spring   /

Fall   /

Year/s

Varieties

....

Sources

....

Date	Notes on Seed Starting, Cultivation, Harvest, Yield, and Flavor

Brussels Sprouts

Brassica oleracea var. *gemmifera*

Be Patient for Brussels Sprouts

Brussels sprouts take 100 days to mature, and they don't like extreme heat, so count back from your expected hard frost in fall for the date to set them out. In short-season areas, that will be spring, but in warmer areas, it may be midsummer. In extremely hot summers, it may be impossible to get a decent crop, so don't blame yourself if yours fails.

Wait until after frost to harvest because the flavor improves with cold. Pick sprouts from the bottom of the stem upward. Plants are very cold hardy and will continue to form new sprouts higher up the stem well into winter.

Those big stalks of sprouts you sometimes see in specialty groceries or farmers' markets? Those were topped a month earlier to stop new growth and allow all the existing sprouts to reach the same size.

TP or DS: Transplant

Start seed: 4 months before average date of first fall frost

Seed depth: ¼"

Germination temperature: 70°F/21°C

Days to germination: 10

Growing temperature: 50 to 60°F/10 to 15°C

Transplant date: 3 months before average date of first fall frost

Spacing: 2' in row; 3' between rows

Ideal Seed-Starting Dates

Spring   /

Fall   /

Year/s

Varieties

....

Sources

....

Date	Notes on Seed Starting, Cultivation, Harvest, Yield, and Flavor

Cabbage

Brassica oleracea var. *capitata*

Keep It Cool

Cabbage can tolerate temperatures as low as 15°F (–9°C), but is intolerant of heat. In areas with hot summers, cabbage should be grown in spring and fall. In areas with cool summers, it can be succession planted all season. Closer spacing produces smaller heads, which may be a plus in a small family.

A Cousin for All Seasons

Chinese cabbage is a different species (*Brassica rapa* var. *pekinensis*) and should be grown more like lettuce. It will bolt if exposed to cold temperatures, so wait until the average date of final spring frost to plant it outside. It is much more tolerant of summer heat and can therefore be succession planted. It is an excellent choice for a fall crop although it can tolerate only a light frost, so count back 60 days from your first frost to find your best planting date.

TP or DS: Transplant

Start seed: 8–10 weeks before average date of final spring frost; 10 weeks before average date of first fall frost

Seed depth: ¼"

Germination temperature: 70°F/21°C

Days to germination: 10

Growing temperature: 50 to 60°F/ 10 to 15°C

Transplant date: 4 weeks before average date of final spring frost; 6 weeks before average date of first fall frost

Spacing: 12–18" in row; 3' between rows

Ideal Seed-Starting Dates

Spring   /   Fall   /   Year/s

Varieties

....

Sources

....

Date	Notes on Seed Starting, Cultivation, Harvest, Yield, and Flavor

Carrots

Daucus carota var. *sativus*

Good Prep for Better Roots

Take the time to prepare the soil well in the carrot bed by removing any stones or clods that might cause the roots to be misshapen. Water the soil well before planting and plan to keep the soil surface moist until germination, which can be as long as 2 to 3 weeks. Add some radish seeds to the carrot seeds when planting—radishes germinate before carrots and prevent the soil from crusting. (Pull the radishes before they size up and compete with the carrots.)

Fall Is Sweet

Sow several times in spring and make a bigger planting for fall. Carrots get sweeter in cold weather. Carrot tops can tolerate only a light frost, but mature roots can be left in the ground and harvested throughout winter, if mulched heavily before the ground freezes.

If the carrots' shoulders start to show at soil level, hill soil around them to prevent them from getting green and bitter at the top.

TP or DS: Direct seed

Start seed: 3–4 weeks before average date of final spring frost; 10–12 weeks before average date of first fall frost

Seed depth: ¼"

Germination temperature: >45°F/7°C

Days to germination: 14–21

Growing temperature: 55 to 60°F/13 to 15°C

Transplant date: N/A

Spacing: 2" apart in wide rows; 2' between rows

Ideal Seed-Starting Dates

Spring   /   Fall   /   **Year/s**

Varieties

....

Sources

....

Date	Notes on Seed Starting, Cultivation, Harvest, Yield, and Flavor

Chicory

Dandelion, endive, radicchio, and other relatives; *Cichorium intybus, C. endivia*

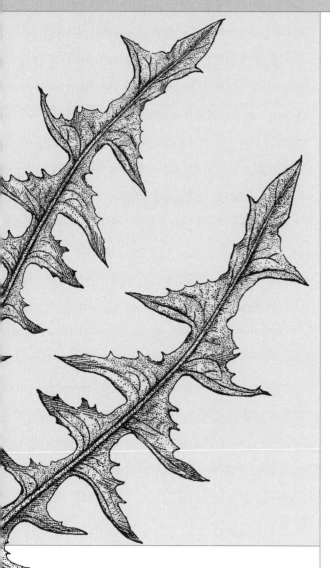

TP or DS: Direct seed leaf types, transplant heading types

Start seed: Direct seed 2–3 weeks before average date of final spring frost; start transplants 6–7 weeks before average date of first fall frost

Seed depth: ¼"

Germination temperature: 70°F/21°C

Days to germination: 7–14

Growing temperature: 55 to 60°F/13 to 15°C

Transplant date: On average date of final spring frost

Spacing: 12" in row; 18" between rows

A Bitter Family

Bitter greens are important in many cuisines, as they are believed to help with digestion. Although not as widely used in North America as elsewhere, chicory is increasing in popularity and merits some trialing by adventurous eaters.

This vast group of salad plants includes endive, escarole, radicchio, radichetta, dandelion, and numerous other varieties.

Leaf chicories. The easiest to grow are the leaf chicories, which can be direct seeded and harvested small like baby lettuce.

Heading chicories. The heading types should be grown like head lettuce, although they are more finicky and less uniform. They require cool weather (<60°F/15°C); in warm weather, the heading types can be quite bitter and bolt quickly. However, low temperatures when young also can cause bolting, so for most climates, fall crops are most successful.

Endive and escarole. These are more tolerant of varying temperatures but do best in cool conditions.

Radicchio. This is the trickiest chicory. In general, older varieties should be planted in spring and cut back in late summer; a new head will grow in fall and that's the one to cut for the best flavor. Newer varieties don't need to be cut back to form the edible head.

Whatever varieties you grow, follow the directions from the seed supplier. If at first you don't succeed, try again in fall because these are all plants that love cool weather, and they vary in their tolerance to frost. Finding those that do well in your climate will be a garden triumph!

Ideal Seed-Starting Dates

Spring   /

Fall   /

Year/s

Varieties

....

Sources

....

Date	Notes on Seed Starting, Cultivation, Harvest, Yield, and Flavor

Collards and Kale

Brassica oleracea var. *acephala*

Versatile Leafy Greens

Collards and kale are similar in their growing requirements, nutritional value, and flavor. Collards have flat, smooth leaves and kale has crinkled or frilly leaves, depending on the variety. All collards are green, whereas kale varieties can be blue, dark green, or violet.

Both can be grown in early spring and late fall, even into winter in a cold frame or under row cover. A light frost improves flavor.

For spring, start the seed indoors because germination can take too long in cold soil. Then transplant hardened-off plants a month before the average date of final spring frost. For fall, you can direct seed 3 to 4 months before hard frost.

Leave More Space for Bigger Plants

The big range in spacing recommendations is based on how you like to use the leaves. Some people harvest the entire plant when it is half grown, whereas others like the plants to get as large as possible so they can pick individual leaves over a long period of time. If you're in the latter category, pick leaves from the bottom. Over time, the plants will look like little palm trees with a tuft of leaves atop the stems. They can reach 3 feet tall and be top-heavy, so always water them to a depth of 6 inches to encourage deep roots.

TP or DS: Transplant for spring, direct seed for fall

Start seed: 8 weeks before average date of final spring frost; 12-16 weeks before average date of first fall frost

Seed depth: ½"

Germination temperature: 70°F/21°C

Days to germination: 4-7

Growing temperature: 50 to 60°F/10 to 15°C

Transplant date: 4 weeks before average date of final spring frost

Spacing: 6-18" in row; 18" between rows

Deep roots will help anchor a big plant, so water kale and collard plants thoroughly.

Ideal Seed-Starting Dates

Spring   /   Fall   /   Year/s

Varieties

....

Sources

....

Date	Notes on Seed Starting, Cultivation, Harvest, Yield, and Flavor

Corn

Zea mays

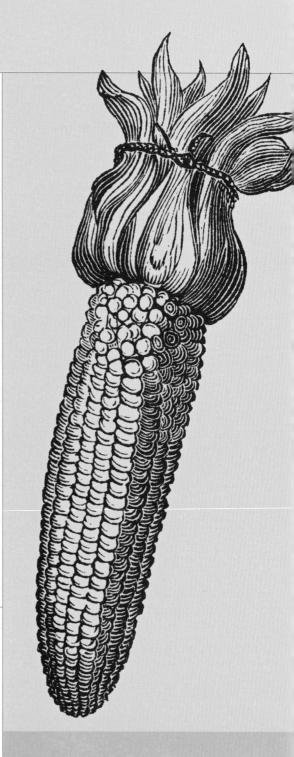

Strategic Planting

For better pollination. Always plant sweet corn in blocks of at least four rows, rather than in a single long row, to aid pollination. To ensure a solid block of plants, plant seeds 4 to 6 inches apart, then thin to about 12 inches apart when the plants are 4 inches tall.

For a long harvest. Supersweet varieties must be kept separate from non-supersweet varieties because cross-pollination between the two types will produce tough, inedible kernels.

To prevent cross-pollination and have corn over a long season, choose several varieties that mature at least 12 days apart. Make a first planting of an early-season variety, wait 2 weeks, then make a second planting of that variety plus a mid- and late-season variety. Repeat.

For companion planting. For a traditional Three Sisters planting of corn, beans, and squash, choose a type such as popcorn or ornamental corn that is left to dry on the plant so you don't have to step on the beans and squash to harvest the corn.

TP or DS: Direct seed

Start seed: Only when soil temperature is >65°F/18°C

Seed depth: 1"

Germination temperature: >65°F/18°C

Days to germination: 7–10

Growing temperature: >60°F/15°C

Transplant date: See note at right

Spacing: 12" between plants; 30–36" between rows

If spring is cold, start seeds indoors 2 to 4 weeks before your average date of final spring frost and plant outside shortly after it.

Ideal Seed-Starting Dates

Spring   /   Fall   /   **Year/s**

Varieties

....

Sources

....

Date	Notes on Seed Starting, Cultivation, Harvest, Yield, and Flavor

Cucumbers

Cucumis sativus

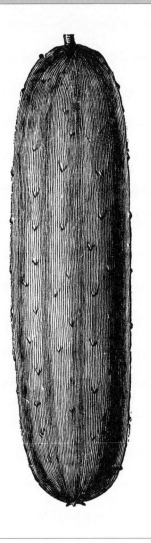

TP or DS: Transplant

Start seed: 2 weeks before average date of final spring frost

Seed depth: 1"

Germination temperature: 72°F/22°C

Days to germination: 3–10

Growing temperature: 60°F/15°C

Transplant date: 2 weeks after average date of final spring frost

Spacing: 12" in row; 6' between rows

Know Your Types

When choosing varieties, pay attention to the terminology in the description. Cucumbers are categorized as monoecious, gynoecious, and parthenocarpic.

Monoecious. These common types produce male and female flowers on the same plant. Male flowers, which produce the pollen, appear first; female flowers, which produce fruits, come later, so you may have to wait a week or two before pollination occurs and fruits form.

Gynoecious. These varieties have more female flowers—and hence more fruits—but you still need some male flowers nearby to provide pollen. These are usually packaged with a few seeds of pollinizer plants marked with a dye. Be sure to plant them or you won't get any cucumbers.

Parthenocarpic. These don't require pollination to produce fruits and are usually the best varieties to grow in a greenhouse.

Start Indoors and Wait for Warmth

Cucumbers require patience. They cannot tolerate cold, so starting plants indoors is the best option. If you choose to direct seed in the garden, wait until the soil temperature is above 65°F (18°C). Don't rush to plant, and don't expect fruits to form as soon as you see flowers.

For clean, straight fruits, grow cucumbers on a fence or trellis; install the structure first so you don't harm the plants' roots.

Ideal Seed-Starting Dates

Spring   /   Fall   /   **Year/s**

Varieties

....

Sources

....

Date	Notes on Seed Starting, Cultivation, Harvest, Yield, and Flavor

Eggplant

Solanum melongena

Getting Off to a Good Start

Eggplant does not like cool weather, so wait until temperatures warm before planting. A heavy feeder, eggplant will do best in well-composted soil and should be given liquid fertilizer when it starts to bloom. It has shallow roots, so be careful when hoeing around plants.

Grow to Avoid Bitterness

Bitterness in eggplant is caused by two factors: insufficient watering and harvesting at the wrong time. To grow eggplant well, you must provide constant moisture to the roots, so mulch the plants and check soil moisture often. To tell if an eggplant is ready to harvest, look for glossy skin of the correct color for the variety you're growing. Press your thumb gently into the fruit; if the flesh compresses then bounces back, it's ready. If it doesn't compress, it's immature. If the depression remains, it is overly mature and not fit to eat, but you should cut off the fruit so the plant will continue to flower.

TP or DS: Transplant

Start seed: 6 weeks before average date of final spring frost

Seed depth: ¼"

Germination temperature: 80 to 90°F/ 27 to 32°C

Days to germination: 7–14

Growing temperature: 60°F/15°C

Transplant date: 2–3 weeks after average date of final spring frost

Spacing: 2' in row; 3' between rows

Eggplant has thorns on the stem, so take care when harvesting!

Ideal Seed-Starting Dates

Spring   /

Fall   /

Year/s

Varieties

....

Sources

....

Date	Notes on Seed Starting, Cultivation, Harvest, Yield, and Flavor

Fennel

Foeniculum vulgare

Crisp Bulbs

Bulb fennel goes by many names: finocchio, Florence fennel, and sweet anise fennel. It has a delicious mild anise flavor and crisp flesh when grown well. Bulb fennel will bolt if it's too hot, too cold, or too dry. Keep the plant moist and growing rapidly, and harvest at the first sign of flower stalks.

Sweet Fronds

Herb fennel will get up to 5 feet tall and will not form a bulb. It can be invasive, so keep an eye on it and cut it back when flower stalks form if you don't want it to self-seed. Use the ferny foliage for fish and potato dishes.

Fragrant Flowers

Fennel flowers also make fragrant additions to bouquets, and there are varieties with bronze foliage that are especially beautiful for cutting. Let some flowers go to seed, and harvest the mature seeds for culinary use.

Harvest the pollen, an expensive gourmet flavoring in Mediterranean cuisine, by shaking the flowers into a bag when the pollen is visible. Or cut the flowers and hang them upside down with a bag over them.

Once you succeed with spring fennel, try a fall crop. Start seeds inside 16 to 18 weeks before the first light frost.

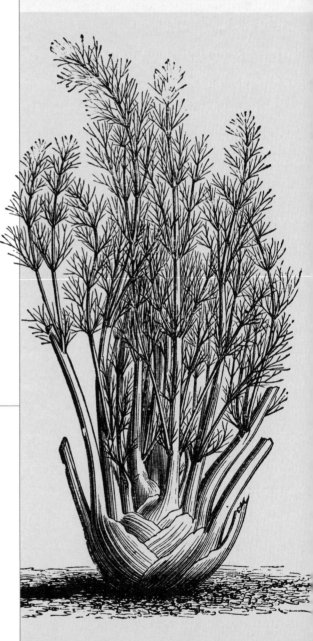

TP or DS: Transplant

Start seed: 6 weeks before average date of final spring frost

Seed depth: ¼"

Germination temperature: 70°F/21°C

Days to germination: 7–10

Growing temperature: 60°F/15°C

Transplant date: Average date of final spring frost

Spacing: 12" in row; 18" between rows

Ideal Seed-Starting Dates

Spring   /   Fall   /   **Year/s**

Varieties

....

Sources

....

Date	Notes on Seed Starting, Cultivation, Harvest, Yield, and Flavor

Garlic

Allium sativum

Choosing a Variety

There are hundreds of named varieties of garlic, divided into two categories: hardneck and softneck types. Hardneck varieties have stronger flavor and easy-to-peel large cloves, but they don't store as long as softnecks. Softnecks have a milder flavor and many small cloves, and they store longer. Hardnecks are very cold hardy and recommended for the extreme North. Softnecks do better in milder winters. Rocambole, a type of hardneck, is not recommended for the South, but other varieties may do fine wherever they are planted.

Grocery store garlic, usually softneck varieties, should not be planted because it may have been treated to inhibit sprouting. Instead, buy seed garlic from a reputable seed company or farmers' market.

Seasonal Timeline

Fall. Garlic should be grown from cloves planted in fall, a few weeks after the first frost but before the ground freezes. One pound of garlic should produce 5 to 7 pounds of bulbs. The plants require at least 40 days of temperatures below 40°F (4°C) or they will not form cloves. That's why fall planting is recommended almost everywhere in the United States and Canada, although gardeners in California and the South may succeed with a January or February planting.

Garlic develops roots after planting and may even produce some foliage in fall. If it dies down over winter, don't be alarmed— it will green up in spring.

Choose a location with well-drained, loose soil; raised beds are ideal. At planting time, break apart the bulbs into cloves, leaving the paper wrappers on them. Plant with tips up and cover with 2 inches of soil above the tips. Water and cover with 3 to 6 inches of mulch to protect the soil over winter.

Spring. In spring, young shoots will poke through the mulch. If it's a cold or wet spring, pull the mulch aside until the garlic plants have emerged. If the spring is dry, water the beds. With hardneck garlic in the North, the main shoot will curl and have a single seed at the tip. These are called scapes. Cut them off when they form (and eat them!), because you will get larger bulbs if you do.

Summer. Garlic leaves will stop growing around the summer solstice and put their energy into the bulbs. When the lower leaves turn brown, it's time to dig the bulbs. Softneck varieties are generally ready for harvest sooner than hardnecks.

Garlic needs to be cured in a dry, well-ventilated place for several weeks. You can hang it in bunches or spread it on racks. Once it's cured, store in a cool, dry place.

TP or DS: Direct sow individual cloves in fall

Start seed: N/A

Seed depth: N/A

Germination temperature: N/A

Days to germination: N/A

Growing temperature: N/A

Transplant date: N/A

Spacing: Plant cloves 4–6" apart in row; 15–24" between rows

Ideal Seed-Starting Dates

Spring /	Fall /	**Year/s**

Varieties

....

Sources

....

Date	Notes on Seed Starting, Cultivation, Harvest, Yield, and Flavor

Leeks

Allium ampeloprasum var. *porrum*

A Slow Crop That Endures

Leeks are a long, slow crop—but worth the effort, because they hold well after harvest. When you start seeds, don't plant them too thickly or the seedlings will be thin and wispy. The ideal size for transplanting to the garden is about the diameter of a pencil. Smaller plants will usually survive if you keep them well watered and weeded.

Grow for Long, White Stems

Leeks should be hilled up as they grow (hoe soil up around the plant; this creates more of the white, edible part). Or try the dibble method: Make a 6-inch-deep hole with a rod slightly bigger than the diameter of your seedlings and plant them with only an inch or two of leaves above the soil. Leeks need constant moisture and appreciate a mulch.

TP or DS: Transplant

Start seed: 12 weeks before average date of final spring frost

Seed depth: 1/8"

Germination temperature: 75°F/24°C

Days to germination: 7–10

Growing temperature: 60°F/15°C

Transplant date: Average date of final spring frost

Spacing: 6" in row; 12" between rows

Ideal Seed-Starting Dates

Spring   /

Fall   /

Year/s

Varieties

....

Sources

....

Date	Notes on Seed Starting, Cultivation, Harvest, Yield, and Flavor

Lettuce

Lactuca sativa

Mixed Planting for Longer Harvest

By growing both a baby lettuce salad mix and a head lettuce, you can have lettuce for months in spring. Six weeks before your average date of final spring frost, start your head lettuce indoors. Start another succession 2 weeks later and, at the same time, direct seed a salad mix outside. By the time the average date of final spring frost arrives, you should be able to cut from the patch of salad mix. You can then plant the head lettuce plants outside. The salad mix should be finishing up right when it's time to pick the head lettuces.

Start your fall lettuce crop 8 to 10 weeks before the average first light frost and keep row cover handy. Mature lettuce is not as frost tolerant as young lettuce.

Choosing Varieties

There are well over 500 lettuce varieties, divided into four basic categories: looseleaf, romaine, butterhead, and crisphead. Some fall between categories. The looseleaf varieties are the quickest, the crispheads the slowest, so choose types based on how long cool weather will last.

Lettuce is a cool-weather crop that can be grown spring and fall in most places, or all summer in cool weather.

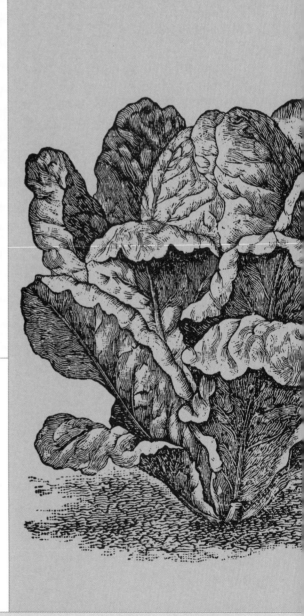

TP or DS: Transplant or direct seed

Start seed: 6–8 weeks before average date of final spring frost

Seed depth: Barely cover with soil or vermiculite

Germination temperature: 75°F/24°C

Days to germination: 2–7

Growing temperature: 55°F/13°C

Transplant date: 3–4 weeks before average date of final spring frost

Spacing: 10" in row; 12" between rows

Ideal Seed-Starting Dates

Spring   /   Fall   /   Year/s

Varieties

....

Sources

....

Date	Notes on Seed Starting, Cultivation, Harvest, Yield, and Flavor

Melons and Watermelons

Cucumis melo, Citrullus lanatus

Give Them Heat

Melons and watermelons like it hot, so don't rush to plant them. When choosing varieties, consider the size of your garden (vining types take a lot of space) and the length of your warm season (some varieties take 140 days to mature). In cool, short-season areas, melons do best when grown on black plastic mulch and covered with row cover until female flowers appear.

Boost Your Harvest

Insect pollination is the most important factor in production. If it's cold and rainy, pollination may be inadequate. Melons and watermelons produce 2 to 5 fruits per plant. Extend the season by succession planting or choosing a few varieties with different days to maturity.

TP or DS: Transplant

Start seed: 2 weeks before average date of final spring frost

Seed depth: ½–1"

Germination temperature: 80°F/27°C

Days to germination: 3–10

Growing temperature: 75°F/24°C

Transplant date: 2 weeks after average date of final spring frost

Spacing: 18" in row; 5' between rows

Small-fruited varieties can be grown on a trellis. Pinch the vine when it reaches the top of the trellis, and support each melon with a net sling.

Ideal Seed-Starting Dates

Spring   /   Fall   /   Year/s

Varieties

....

Sources

....

Date	Notes on Seed Starting, Cultivation, Harvest, Yield, and Flavor

Okra

Abelmoschus esculentus

Grow for Pods and Flowers

Okra is one of those vegetables you either love or hate. But even if you don't like the flavor or mucilaginous texture, you may want to grow okra for its ornamental value. Tall plants with large leaves and yellow hibiscus-like flowers give a tropical presence in the garden.

Pick Early, Pick Often

For eating, the pods should be picked just 4 days after the flower opens, when 2 to 4 inches long. Picking daily will keep the plants producing, but toward the end of the season, you may want to leave some pods to mature and become woody, textural works of art. Think about using them for fall decorations or holiday crafts.

Okra is a tropical plant, so don't plant until the soil temperature is 65°F/18°C. Soaking the seed overnight will speed germination.

TP or DS: Transplant or direct seed

Start seed: 4–6 weeks before average date of final spring frost

Seed depth: ½"

Germination temperature: 75°F/24°C

Days to germination: 5–10

Growing temperature: 70°F/21°C

Transplant date: When soil temperature is >65°F/18°C

Spacing: 12" in row; 3' between rows

Ideal Seed-Starting Dates

Spring   /

Fall   /

Year/s

Varieties

....

Sources

....

Date	Notes on Seed Starting, Cultivation, Harvest, Yield, and Flavor

Onions

Allium cepa

Start from Seed

Onions are most easily grown from purchased sets or plants, but variety selection may be limited, and it's really not hard to grow them from seed. Plant them in cell flats, 4 or 5 seeds per cell, or sprinkle the seed into an open flat. They germinate quickly and will soon be so tall the tops may fall over. When that happens, cut the tops off with scissors to about 4 inches tall. A second trim right before planting is fine, too.

Good Growing

Onions can be planted singly or in clumps of 3 or 4 seedlings, but allow more space between clumps. Keep well watered, as the roots are shallow. Pull when the tops fall over, and leave the onions in the sun to cure for a few days.

Green onions are just immature bulbing onions.

TP or DS: Transplant

Start seed: 10 weeks before average date of final spring frost

Seed depth: ⅛"

Germination temperature: 75°F/24°C

Days to germination: 4–5

Growing temperature: 60°F/15°C

Transplant date: 2–4 weeks before average date of final spring frost

Spacing: 4" in row; 12" between rows

Ideal Seed-Starting Dates

Spring   /

Fall   /

Year/s

Varieties

....

Sources

....

Date	Notes on Seed Starting, Cultivation, Harvest, Yield, and Flavor

Parsley

Petroselinum crispum

Choose Your Leaf Style

Curled or flat leaf? It's a matter of taste or, to be more precise, "mouthfeel." (Some people dislike anything fuzzy in the mouth.) Otherwise, the two types are grown the same way.

Slow but Easy

Apart from its very long time to germination—up to 3 weeks—parsley is easy to grow. It is both cold and heat tolerant, so it can be started inside and set out early. Individual stems can be harvested as soon and as often as needed. It can be left in the garden late and usually will survive well into winter.

Grow for Pollinators

Parsley is also a great plant for a pollinator garden because it is a host plant for black swallowtail butterflies. Grow plenty and don't worry when parsleyworms start to munch it—they will soon turn into butterflies and fly away, and the plants will recover.

Parsley is a biennial that may overwinter in mild areas. In its second year, the new growth will be fine for eating but once it flowers, the leaves turn bitter.

TP or DS: Transplant

Start seed: 9–10 weeks before average date of final spring frost

Seed depth: ¼"

Germination temperature: 70°F/21°C

Days to germination: 15–21

Growing temperature: 60°F/15°C

Transplant date: 2–3 weeks before average date of final spring frost

Spacing: 12" in row

Ideal Seed-Starting Dates

Spring   /   Fall   /   **Year/s**

Varieties

....

Sources

....

Date	Notes on Seed Starting, Cultivation, Harvest, Yield, and Flavor

Parsnips

Pastinaca sativa

Long, Sweet Roots

Parsnips take 4 months to mature and will taste best after they have been kissed by a few frosts. You can even leave them in the ground all winter and harvest as you need them, provided you have mulched heavily before cold weather arrives. Interplant in spring with vegetables that will be harvested early, such as lettuce and radishes.

Soak Seeds to Speed Germination

Parsnip seeds are slow to germinate, taking up to 4 weeks in cold soil. To speed germination, soak them overnight before planting and plant a few radish seeds with them to mark the row and prevent the soil from crusting. Hill up as the roots grow to prevent greening of the shoulders.

Let your soil type guide your variety decisions; if you have hard clay soil, choose a short, blocky cultivar.

Parsnips will be in the garden all season, so choose a spot where they won't be disturbed. And be sure to thin plants to the recommended spacing; otherwise, root quality will suffer.

TP or DS: Direct seed

Start seed: On average date of final spring frost or later for fall harvest

Seed depth: ½"

Germination temperature: 60°F/15°C

Days to germination: 14–21 days

Growing temperature: 60°F/15°C

Transplant date: N/A

Spacing: 3" in row; 18" between rows

Ideal Seed-Starting Dates

Spring   /   Fall   /   **Year/s**

Varieties

....

Sources

....

Date	Notes on Seed Starting, Cultivation, Harvest, Yield, and Flavor

Peas

Pisum sativum

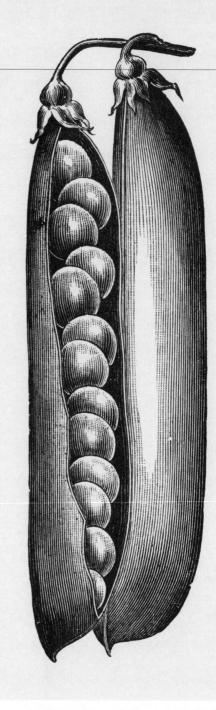

Shelling, Snap, and Snow

Shelling peas fresh from the garden is one of life's quiet pleasures. Enjoy the satisfying snap of the pod as you break it open to reveal the brilliant green gems within. You may prefer the efficiency of edible-podded snow and snap peas, though. Snow peas are picked when the seeds inside are small and flat. Snap peas, also called sugar snap peas, are picked when the seeds are enlarged but before the pod gets tough.

Choosing Varieties

Consider height when choosing varieties—the range is considerable, with some heirlooms growing over 6 feet and requiring a robust trellis. Pay attention to days to maturity, because some dwarf varieties will bear a month earlier than tall ones, an important consideration where hot weather arrives early. Peas do not like heat.

TP or DS: Direct seed

Start seed: 6 weeks before average date of final spring frost

Seed depth: 1"

Germination temperature: 50°F/10°C

Days to germination: 7–14 days

Growing temperature: Peas are cold tolerant once up but require soil temperature >50°F/10°C

Transplant date: N/A

Spacing: 3" in row; 18" between rows

Peas are legumes that fix nitrogen from the air and therefore do not need nitrogen fertilizer. Too much nitrogen will cause lush foliage with few peas.

Ideal Seed-Starting Dates

Spring   /   Fall   /

Year/s

Varieties

....

Sources

....

Date	Notes on Seed Starting, Cultivation, Harvest, Yield, and Flavor

Peppers

Capsicum annuum

Growing the Best Peppers

Wait for warmth. Like most warm-weather crops, peppers should not be rushed into the garden. Cold weather early on may set them back, and they may never fully recover. It's better to be patient and keep them indoors until the weather is warm and settled.

Transition to the garden. Unlike some other crops, peppers don't want a long period of hardening off. Just a few days with reduced water at 60°F (15°C) will make them garden ready.

Little nitrogen, consistent water. Peppers are modest feeders, and a lot of nitrogen will result in too much foliage and not much fruit. Consistent soil moisture will provide the best production, and some tall varieties will benefit from a cage or stake. In midsummer, warm night temperatures may reduce fruit set, but plants will recover when nights turn cooler.

TP or DS: Transplant

Start seed: 8 weeks before average date of final spring frost

Seed depth: ¼"

Germination temperature: 80 to 90°F/ 27 to 32°C

Days to germination: 10

Growing temperature: 70°F/21°C

Transplant date: 2–3 weeks after average date of final spring frost

Spacing: 18" in row; 2–3' between rows

Harvest all peppers with scissors to avoid breaking the stems. Be especially careful when handling hot peppers, as the heat compounds can burn skin and eyes.

Ideal Seed-Starting Dates

Spring   /   Fall   /   **Year/s**

Varieties

....

Sources

....

Date	Notes on Seed Starting, Cultivation, Harvest, Yield, and Flavor

Potatoes

Solanum tuberosum

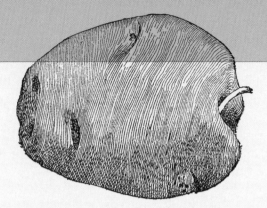

Potatoes are grown from pieces of seed potatoes, which should be purchased from a reputable supplier to ensure they are certified disease-free. Local nurseries may have a half-dozen varieties, but there are online specialists with a much wider selection. One pound will produce 3 to 10 pounds of potatoes, depending on variety and conditions.

Planting Spuds

Seed potatoes the size of a chicken egg or smaller can be planted whole. Larger potatoes should be cut into pieces with two eyes or buds. To prevent the pieces from rotting in the soil, you can put them in a brown paper bag with the top closed and leave them at room temperature for 2 to 4 days until the cut sides are callused.

Wait until soil has reached 40°F (4°C) before cutting seed pieces. When you are ready to plant, dig a trench 4 inches deep and place the seed pieces, eyes up, 8 to 12 inches apart with rows 2 to 3 feet apart. Rake soil over them and water if the soil is dry. Sprouts will emerge in 2 to 4 weeks, depending on the soil temperature.

Potatoes are modest feeders; too much fertilizer can cause excessive foliar growth at the expense of tuber production. They prefer an acidic soil; a high pH can lead to scab on the potatoes, so look for scab-resistant varieties if your soil is very alkaline.

Hill Your Tubers

Potatoes should be either hilled or mulched as they grow, to prevent sunlight from reaching the tubers, which can turn them green and bitter. To hill potatoes, wait until the plants are about 8 inches tall and hoe soil up around the stem to within an inch of the lowest leaves. Repeat several times as the plants grow—you will have a ridge along your potato row. Or you can pull mulch around the stems, leaving the foliage exposed to sun but covering the soil surface.

As anyone who has had potato plants in their compost knows, potatoes can be grown in many different situations, including buckets, tall wire cages filled with straw, and felt planters. However you grow your main crop, plant a few pieces in your best garden soil so you can dig them up easily as small "new potatoes." With luck, they'll be ready the same time as garden peas, giving you one of the most iconic meals of the gardening year.

TP or DS: Direct sow seed potatoes or pieces

Start seed: When soil temperature reaches 40°F (4°C)

Seed depth: 4"

Germination temperature: N/A

Days to germination: N/A

Growing temperature: N/A

Transplant date: N/A

Spacing: 8–12" in row; 2–3' between rows

Ideal Seed-Starting Dates

Spring   /   Fall   /

Year/s

Varieties

....

Sources

....

Date	Notes on Seed Starting, Cultivation, Harvest, Yield, and Flavor

Radishes

Raphanus sativus

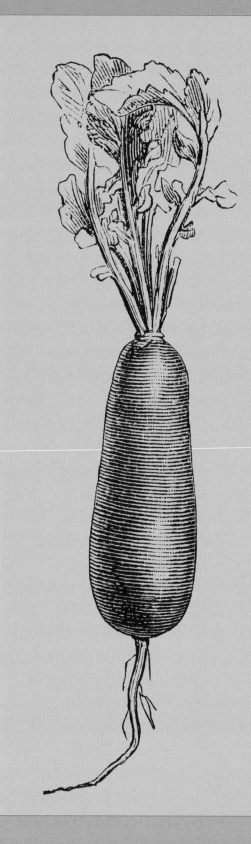

Choose Your Variety

With more than 250 cultivars, everyone should be able to find one that is pleasing. Spring radishes, the quickest crop at just 30 days to maturity, are often the spiciest. The huge daikon radish takes at least twice as long to mature and is usually the mildest. Available in numerous shapes, colors, and sizes, radishes are well worth a few trials.

Plant Often, Water Well

Plant radishes every 2 weeks in the amount you want to eat; they don't hold well in the ground, turning hot and pithy if too mature. Keep them evenly moist and harvest as soon as they reach the predicted size for the variety. Radishes are often planted with slower-germinating seeds such as carrots to mark the rows and keep the soil from crusting.

Eat the Pods

As the temperature warms, radishes quickly go to seed. You can eat the seed pods, or harvest the seed to plant in fall for spicy microgreens.

TP or DS: Direct seed

Start seed: As soon as the soil can be worked in spring

Seed depth: ½"

Germination temperature: 50°F/10°C

Days to germination: 5 days

Growing temperature: >50°F/10°C

Transplant date: N/A

Spacing: 1" in row; 12" between rows

Ideal Seed-Starting Dates

Spring   /

Fall   /

Year/s

Varieties

....

Sources

....

Date	Notes on Seed Starting, Cultivation, Harvest, Yield, and Flavor

Salad Mix and Baby Greens

Multiple species

This is a catchall category for gardeners who like to start eating soon after planting. All kinds of leafy greens can be part of a salad mix or harvested as baby greens: arugula, brassicas, chicory, lettuce, mâche, spinach, and so on. You can purchase seed mixes— "mesclun" in French, "misticanza" in Italian—selected to provide color, texture, and compatible days to harvest. Or you can create your own mix using varieties you particularly like that do especially well for you.

Make Your Own Leafy Green Mix

You also can mix together leftover seed from previous leafy green plantings. Virtually anything in the leafy green category can be picked and eaten within 30 days of planting, and many can be cut off at the crown to resprout and provide a second cutting. Or you can pull individual plants as baby greens, effectively thinning those that remain to grow to a larger size.

Growing Microgreens

Microgreens are harvested just before the first true leaves emerge and are a great option for growing indoors when it's cold outside. Fill a shallow tray with planting mix and sprinkle seeds thickly, then cover with soil mix or vermiculite. Bottom water to prevent soil from splashing onto emerging seedlings. When the seedlings have fully developed cotyledons (the first set of leaves), cut the sprouts with scissors and enjoy the boost of flavor and nutrition.

TP or DS: Direct seed

Start seed: Direct seed 2–3 weeks before average date of final spring frost

Seed depth: ¼"

Germination temperature: 70°F/21°C

Days to germination: 7–14

Growing temperature: 55 to 60°F/13 to 15°C

Transplant date: N/A

Spacing: Seed in bands or blocks, aiming for 1" spacing

To keep salad mix in the fridge for up to 2 weeks, cut the leaves when they are crisp, wash and spin-dry them immediately, and store them loosely, not packed tight, in a bag or airtight container.

Ideal Seed-Starting Dates

Spring   /   Fall   /   Year/s

Varieties

....

Sources

....

Date	Notes on Seed Starting, Cultivation, Harvest, Yield, and Flavor

Spinach

Spinacia oleracea

Spinach is a cool-weather crop and should be planted every 2 weeks from early spring until the average date of final spring frost then again in fall when the weather starts to cool off. In cold climates, a little protection such as a cold frame or row cover will keep spinach alive almost all winter. Any stress, such as early heat, dry soil, or crowded spacing, will cause spinach to bolt and go to seed. Plant it every week and choose bolt-resistant varieties for later plantings if you want to extend your harvest. However, spinach can be picked as individual leaves as soon as they are large enough to eat, so you can have a fairly long season from a single planting. Spinach can also be planted in late fall and mulched heavily. It will emerge in early spring when conditions are right.

TP or DS: Direct seed

Start seed: As soon as the soil can be worked in spring

Seed depth: ½"

Germination temperature: 50°F/10°C

Days to germination: 5 days

Growing temperature: >50°F/10°C

Transplant date: N/A

Spacing: 1" in row; 12" between rows

Smooth-leaf varieties are best for salads; savoyed types are better for cooking.

Ideal Seed-Starting Dates

Spring   /   Fall   /   **Year/s**

Varieties

....

Sources

....

Date	Notes on Seed Starting, Cultivation, Harvest, Yield, and Flavor

Squash, Summer and Winter

Cucurbita spp.

Beat the Beetles

Squash can be direct seeded, but only after the soil has thoroughly warmed. You may prefer to start seed indoors in a 3- to 4-inch pot so that the plants get a head start before squash bugs and cucumber beetles, squash's biggest challenges, become active.

Eat the Male Flowers

Squash plants produce both male and female flowers. You can easily identify the female flowers because they have little fruits attached to the base. It's common for the plant to initially produce all male flowers, which you can cut and use in squash blossom recipes. Always leave some male flowers to pollinate the female flowers that follow.

Harvest at the Right Time

Pick summer squash small and slender. If one grows into a giant, remove the seeds and grate the flesh for use in baked goods, fritters, and pasta sauce. Success with winter squash and pumpkins lies in harvesting at the correct time, and every type has different requirements. See details from the seed supplier or your Extension office.

TP or DS: Transplant

Start seed: 3–4 weeks before average date of final spring frost

Seed depth: ½"

Germination temperature: 72°F/22°C

Days to germination: 3–10 days

Growing temperature: 62°F/17°C

Transplant date: 1 week after average date of final spring frost

Spacing: 18–24" in row; 6' between rows

If fruits are dropping off or not fully formed, try hand-pollinating: Using a small artist's paintbrush, sweep up pollen from male flowers and deposit it on the female flower's stigma, the sticky knob in the middle of the flower.

Ideal Seed-Starting Dates

Spring   /   Fall   /   Year/s

Varieties

....

Sources

....

Date	Notes on Seed Starting, Cultivation, Harvest, Yield, and Flavor

Sweet Potatoes

Ipomoea batatas

Start with Slips

Sweet potatoes are grown from slips that are purchased from a specialty supplier. It's possible to grow your own slips, but it takes 6 weeks and experience to get it right, so you might want to save that garden adventure until you are experienced with growing the actual crop. Ten successful plants can produce 15 to 30 pounds of sweet potatoes.

Wait for Warm Weather

Sweet potatoes are very tender and require warm weather and a long season (up to 120 days) to grow; they may not be suitable in places with cool summers. Don't rush to plant them. When the soil has warmed to at least 65°F (18°C), plant the slips 12 inches apart in rows 3 to 4 feet apart. Water is important for the first 50 to 60 days after planting; after that, sweet potatoes are tolerant of dry weather.

Weeding is usually necessary only for the first few weeks because the fast-growing vines will shade out competition. After 80 days, check the root size because the tubers will keep growing and could split if you leave them too long. Temperatures below 55°F (13°C) can cause chilling injury, so be ready to harvest as cold weather approaches.

TP or DS: N/A

Start seed: N/A

Seed depth: N/A

Germination temperature: N/A

Days to germination: N/A

Growing temperature: N/A

Transplant date: N/A

Spacing: Plant slips 12" apart in rows; 3–4' between rows

Many people consider sweet potato greens a delicacy. They can be eaten fresh like salad greens or sautéed with other vegetables.

Ideal Seed-Starting Dates

Spring   /   Fall   /   **Year/s**

Varieties

....

Sources

....

Date	Notes on Seed Starting, Cultivation, Harvest, Yield, and Flavor

Swiss Chard

Beta vulgaris

Swiss chard is the same species as beets and has basically the same growing requirements. The seeds come in clusters, so thinning is required after germination, but the thinnings are good in salads. Chard varieties vary in color and in thickness of the stem, which is a matter of preference. Leaves can be harvested individually as needed.

The plants are somewhat heat tolerant and will continue to grow into summer, but they prefer cooler weather. If yours look inedible in summer heat, cut the plants back above the crown. Once the weather cools down, they are likely to get a new lease on life and provide tender greens until hard freeze.

Swiss chard requires nitrogen to produce all those huge leaves, so sidedress the plants or water with compost tea when they are about a month old.

TP or DS: Direct seed

Start seed: 1–2 weeks before average date of final spring frost

Seed depth: ½"

Germination temperature: >45°F/7°C

Days to germination: 7–15

Growing temperature: 55 to 60°F/13 to 15°C

Transplant date: N/A

Spacing: 8" in row; 12" between rows

Ideal Seed-Starting Dates

Spring   /   Fall   /   **Year/s**

Varieties

....

Sources

....

Date	Notes on Seed Starting, Cultivation, Harvest, Yield, and Flavor

Tomatoes

Solanum lycopersicum

Tips and Tricks

Entire books have been written about how to grow a good tomato, and every gardener has some special tricks.

Choose the right variety. Variety selection is important, so start your research at your local Extension office to see which varieties are recommended for your area.

Test your soil. Because flavor is related to soil, get a soil test and request recommendations for growing tomatoes.

Prune and stake. Tomato pruning and trellising can affect your success, so take the time to learn about the various methods and choose the one that works best in your garden. Hint: Those small wire cages from the hardware store aren't sturdy enough to help with anything but the smallest determinate variety.

TP or DS: Transplant

Start seed: 8 weeks before average date of final spring frost

Seed depth: ⅛"

Germination temperature: 75°F/24°C

Days to germination: 7–14

Growing temperature: 70°F/21°C

Transplant date: 2–3 weeks after average date of final spring frost

Spacing: 12–24" for determinate varieties; 24–36" for indeterminate

Tomato maturity is often described in more general terms than other vegetables. Early varieties take up to 65 days; midseason are 66 to 79 days; and late are 80 days plus.

Ideal Seed-Starting Dates

Spring   /   Fall   /   **Year/s**

Varieties

....

Sources

....

Date	Notes on Seed Starting, Cultivation, Harvest, Yield, and Flavor

Record Sheets

Use this space to continue your records for each vegetable
you've started tracking, or use it to add new crops
you've never tried before.

Crop: ....

Year/s

Ideal Seed-Starting Dates Spring   /   Fall   /

Varieties

....

....

Sources

....

....

Date	Notes on Seed Starting, Cultivation, Harvest, Yield, and Flavor

Crop: ....

Year/s [   ]

Ideal Seed-Starting Dates [Spring   /   ] [Fall   /   ]

Varieties

....

....

Sources

....

....

Date	Notes on Seed Starting, Cultivation, Harvest, Yield, and Flavor
....	
....	
....	
....	
....	
....	
....	
....	
....	
....	
....	
....	
....	
....	
....	
....	
....	
....	

Crop: ....   Year/s [   ]

Ideal Seed-Starting Dates   [Spring   /   ]   [Fall   /   ]

Varieties

....

....

Sources

....

....

Date	Notes on Seed Starting, Cultivation, Harvest, Yield, and Flavor

Crop: ....   Year/s [   ]

Ideal Seed-Starting Dates   [Spring   /   ]   [Fall   /   ]

Varieties

....

....

Sources

....

....

Date	Notes on Seed Starting, Cultivation, Harvest, Yield, and Flavor

Crop: ....   Year/s [   ]

Ideal Seed-Starting Dates   [Spring   /   ]   [Fall   /   ]

Varieties

....

....

Sources

....

....

Date	Notes on Seed Starting, Cultivation, Harvest, Yield, and Flavor

Crop: .... Year/s

Ideal Seed-Starting Dates | Spring   / | Fall   /

Varieties

....

....

Sources

....

....

Date	Notes on Seed Starting, Cultivation, Harvest, Yield, and Flavor

Crop: ....

Year/s [   ]

Ideal Seed-Starting Dates [Spring   /   ] [Fall   /   ]

Varieties

....

....

Sources

....

....

Date	Notes on Seed Starting, Cultivation, Harvest, Yield, and Flavor

Crop: .... Year/s [   ]

Ideal Seed-Starting Dates   Spring   /   Fall   /

Varieties

....

....

Sources

....

....

Date	Notes on Seed Starting, Cultivation, Harvest, Yield, and Flavor

Crop: .... Year/s [   ]

Ideal Seed-Starting Dates   Spring   /   Fall   /

Varieties

....

....

Sources

....

....

Date	Notes on Seed Starting, Cultivation, Harvest, Yield, and Flavor

Crop: ....

Ideal Seed-Starting Dates   Spring   /   Fall   /

Varieties

....

....

Sources

....

....

Date	Notes on Seed Starting, Cultivation, Harvest, Yield, and Flavor

Crop: .... Year/s [   ]

Ideal Seed-Starting Dates | Spring   / | Fall   / |

Varieties

....

....

Sources

....

....

Date	Notes on Seed Starting, Cultivation, Harvest, Yield, and Flavor

Crop: ....

Ideal Seed-Starting Dates   Spring   /   Fall   /

Varieties

....

....

Sources

....

....

Date	Notes on Seed Starting, Cultivation, Harvest, Yield, and Flavor
....	
....	
....	
....	
....	
....	
....	
....	
....	
....	
....	
....	
....	
....	
....	
....	
....	
....	
....	

Crop: .... Year/s [   ]

Ideal Seed-Starting Dates   Spring   /   Fall   /

Varieties

....

....

Sources

....

....

Date	Notes on Seed Starting, Cultivation, Harvest, Yield, and Flavor

Crop: ....

Year/s [   ]

Ideal Seed-Starting Dates | Spring   / | Fall   /

Varieties

....

....

Sources

....

....

Date	Notes on Seed Starting, Cultivation, Harvest, Yield, and Flavor
....	
....	
....	
....	
....	
....	
....	
....	
....	
....	
....	
....	
....	
....	
....	
....	
....	
....	
....	

Crop: .... Year/s

Ideal Seed-Starting Dates   Spring   /   Fall   /

Varieties

....

....

Sources

....

....

Date	Notes on Seed Starting, Cultivation, Harvest, Yield, and Flavor

Crop: .... Year/s

Ideal Seed-Starting Dates | Spring   / | Fall   /

Varieties

....

....

Sources

....

....

Date	Notes on Seed Starting, Cultivation, Harvest, Yield, and Flavor
....	
....	
....	
....	
....	
....	
....	
....	
....	
....	
....	
....	
....	
....	
....	
....	
....	
....	

Crop: .... Year/s

Ideal Seed-Starting Dates   Spring   /   Fall   /

Varieties

....

....

Sources

....

....

Date	Notes on Seed Starting, Cultivation, Harvest, Yield, and Flavor

Crop: .... Year/s [ ]

Ideal Seed-Starting Dates   Spring [/]   Fall [/]

Varieties

....

....

Sources

....

....

Date	Notes on Seed Starting, Cultivation, Harvest, Yield, and Flavor

Crop: ....

Year/s [   ]

Ideal Seed-Starting Dates   Spring [/   ]   Fall [/   ]

Varieties

....

....

Sources

....

....

Date	Notes on Seed Starting, Cultivation, Harvest, Yield, and Flavor

Crop: .... Year/s [ ]

Ideal Seed-Starting Dates | Spring   / | Fall   / |

Varieties

....

....

Sources

....

....

Date	Notes on Seed Starting, Cultivation, Harvest, Yield, and Flavor

Crop: .... Year/s [   ]

Ideal Seed-Starting Dates   [Spring   /   ]   [Fall   /   ]

Varieties

....

....

Sources

....

....

Date	Notes on Seed Starting, Cultivation, Harvest, Yield, and Flavor

Crop: ....

Year/s

Ideal Seed-Starting Dates   Spring   /   Fall   /

Varieties
....
....

Sources
....
....

Date	Notes on Seed Starting, Cultivation, Harvest, Yield, and Flavor

Crop: .... Year/s [   ]

Ideal Seed-Starting Dates | Spring   / | | Fall   / |

Varieties

....

....

Sources

....

....

Date	Notes on Seed Starting, Cultivation, Harvest, Yield, and Flavor

Crop: .... Year/s [   ]

Ideal Seed-Starting Dates   Spring [/   ]   Fall [/   ]

Varieties

....

....

Sources

....

....

Date	Notes on Seed Starting, Cultivation, Harvest, Yield, and Flavor

Crop: .... Year/s [   ]

Ideal Seed-Starting Dates   Spring   /   Fall   /

Varieties

....

....

Sources

....

....

Date	Notes on Seed Starting, Cultivation, Harvest, Yield, and Flavor

Crop: .... Year/s [   ]

Ideal Seed-Starting Dates   Spring   /   Fall   /

Varieties

....

....

Sources

....

....

Date	Notes on Seed Starting, Cultivation, Harvest, Yield, and Flavor

Crop: ....

Year/s [   ]

Ideal Seed-Starting Dates   Spring   /   [   ]   Fall   /   [   ]

Varieties

....

....

Sources

....

....

Date	Notes on Seed Starting, Cultivation, Harvest, Yield, and Flavor
....	
....	
....	
....	
....	
....	
....	
....	
....	
....	
....	
....	
....	
....	
....	
....	
....	
....	

Crop: .... Year/s [   ]

Ideal Seed-Starting Dates   Spring   /   Fall   /

Varieties

....

....

Sources

....

....

Date	Notes on Seed Starting, Cultivation, Harvest, Yield, and Flavor
....	
....	
....	
....	
....	
....	
....	
....	
....	
....	
....	
....	
....	
....	
....	
....	
....	
....	

Crop:

Year/s

Ideal Seed-Starting Dates   Spring   /   Fall   /

Varieties

....

....

Sources

....

....

Date	Notes on Seed Starting, Cultivation, Harvest, Yield, and Flavor

Crop: .... Year/s [   ]

Ideal Seed-Starting Dates   Spring   /   Fall   /

Varieties

....

....

Sources

....

....

Date	Notes on Seed Starting, Cultivation, Harvest, Yield, and Flavor

Crop: .... Year/s [   ]

Ideal Seed-Starting Dates   Spring   /   Fall   /

Varieties

....

....

Sources

....

....

Date	Notes on Seed Starting, Cultivation, Harvest, Yield, and Flavor

Crop: .... Year/s [   ]

Ideal Seed-Starting Dates   Spring   /   Fall   /

Varieties

....

....

Sources

....

....

Date	Notes on Seed Starting, Cultivation, Harvest, Yield, and Flavor
....	
....	
....	
....	
....	
....	
....	
....	
....	
....	
....	
....	
....	
....	
....	
....	
....	
....	
....	

Crop: .... Year/s [   ]

Ideal Seed-Starting Dates   Spring   /   Fall   /

Varieties

....

....

Sources

....

....

Date	Notes on Seed Starting, Cultivation, Harvest, Yield, and Flavor

Crop: .... Year/s [   ]

Ideal Seed-Starting Dates   Spring [/   ]   Fall [/   ]

Varieties

....

....

Sources

....

....

....

Date	Notes on Seed Starting, Cultivation, Harvest, Yield, and Flavor

Crop: .... Year/s [   ]

Ideal Seed-Starting Dates | Spring   / | | Fall   / |

Varieties

....

....

Sources

....

....

Date	Notes on Seed Starting, Cultivation, Harvest, Yield, and Flavor

Crop: ....   Year/s

Ideal Seed-Starting Dates   Spring   /   Fall   /

Varieties

....

....

Sources

....

....

Date	Notes on Seed Starting, Cultivation, Harvest, Yield, and Flavor

Crop: ....

Year/s [   ]

Ideal Seed-Starting Dates   Spring [/   ]   Fall [/   ]

Varieties

....

....

Sources

....

....

Date	Notes on Seed Starting, Cultivation, Harvest, Yield, and Flavor
....	
....	
....	
....	
....	
....	
....	
....	
....	
....	
....	
....	
....	
....	
....	
....	
....	

Crop: .... Year/s [   ]

Ideal Seed-Starting Dates   Spring   /   Fall   /

Varieties

....

....

Sources

....

....

Date	Notes on Seed Starting, Cultivation, Harvest, Yield, and Flavor

Crop: ....

Year/s [   ]

Ideal Seed-Starting Dates Spring [/   ] Fall [/   ]

Varieties

....

....

Sources

....

....

Date	Notes on Seed Starting, Cultivation, Harvest, Yield, and Flavor

Crop: .... Year/s

Ideal Seed-Starting Dates Spring   /   Fall   /

Varieties

....

....

Sources

....

....

Date	Notes on Seed Starting, Cultivation, Harvest, Yield, and Flavor

Crop: ....

Year/s

Ideal Seed-Starting Dates

Spring   /

Fall   /

Varieties
....

....

Sources
....

....

Date	Notes on Seed Starting, Cultivation, Harvest, Yield, and Flavor

Crop: .... Year/s [   ]

Ideal Seed-Starting Dates   Spring   /   Fall   /

Varieties

....

....

Sources

....

....

Date	Notes on Seed Starting, Cultivation, Harvest, Yield, and Flavor

Crop: .... Year/s [   ]

Ideal Seed-Starting Dates   Spring [/   ]   Fall [/   ]

Varieties

....

....

Sources

....

....

Date	Notes on Seed Starting, Cultivation, Harvest, Yield, and Flavor

Crop: .... Year/s [   ]

Ideal Seed-Starting Dates   [Spring   /   ]   [Fall   /   ]

Varieties

....

....

Sources

....

....

Date	Notes on Seed Starting, Cultivation, Harvest, Yield, and Flavor
......	
......	
......	
......	
......	
......	
......	
......	
......	
......	
......	
......	
......	
......	
......	
......	
......	
......	
......	
......	
......	

Crop: .... Year/s [   ]

Ideal Seed-Starting Dates Spring [/   ] Fall [/   ]

Varieties

....

....

Sources

....

....

Date	Notes on Seed Starting, Cultivation, Harvest, Yield, and Flavor
.....	
.....	
.....	
.....	
.....	
.....	
.....	
.....	
.....	
.....	
.....	
.....	
.....	
.....	
.....	
.....	
.....	
.....	
.....	

Crop: .... Year/s [   ]

Ideal Seed-Starting Dates   Spring   /   Fall   /

Varieties

....

....

Sources

....

....

Date	Notes on Seed Starting, Cultivation, Harvest, Yield, and Flavor

Crop: ....

Year/s

Ideal Seed-Starting Dates   Spring   /   Fall   /

Varieties

....

....

Sources

....

....

Date	Notes on Seed Starting, Cultivation, Harvest, Yield, and Flavor

Crop: .... Year/s [   ]

Ideal Seed-Starting Dates [Spring   /   ] [Fall   /   ]

Varieties

....

....

Sources

....

....

Date	Notes on Seed Starting, Cultivation, Harvest, Yield, and Flavor

Crop: ....

Year/s

Ideal Seed-Starting Dates

| Spring / | Fall / |

Varieties

....

....

Sources

....

....

Date	Notes on Seed Starting, Cultivation, Harvest, Yield, and Flavor

Crop: ....

Year/s

Ideal Seed-Starting Dates

Spring   /

Fall   /

Varieties

....

....

Sources

....

....

Date	Notes on Seed Starting, Cultivation, Harvest, Yield, and Flavor

Crop: .... Year/s [   ]

Ideal Seed-Starting Dates   Spring   /   Fall   /

Varieties

....

....

Sources

....

....

Date	Notes on Seed Starting, Cultivation, Harvest, Yield, and Flavor
....	
....	
....	
....	
....	
....	
....	
....	
....	
....	
....	
....	
....	
....	
....	
....	
....	
....	

Crop: .... Year/s

Ideal Seed-Starting Dates   Spring   /   Fall   /

Varieties

....

....

Sources

....

....

Date	Notes on Seed Starting, Cultivation, Harvest, Yield, and Flavor

Crop: ....

Ideal Seed-Starting Dates   Spring   /   Fall   /

Varieties

....

....

Sources

....

....

Date	Notes on Seed Starting, Cultivation, Harvest, Yield, and Flavor

Crop: .... Year/s [   ]

Ideal Seed-Starting Dates Spring [/   ] Fall [/   ]

Varieties

....

....

Sources

....

....

Date	Notes on Seed Starting, Cultivation, Harvest, Yield, and Flavor

Crop: ....

Year/s

Ideal Seed-Starting Dates Spring   /   Fall   /

Varieties

....

....

Sources

....

....

Date	Notes on Seed Starting, Cultivation, Harvest, Yield, and Flavor

Crop: .... Year/s [   ]

Ideal Seed-Starting Dates   Spring   /   Fall   /

Varieties

....

....

Sources

....

....

Date	Notes on Seed Starting, Cultivation, Harvest, Yield, and Flavor

Crop: ....

Year/s

Ideal Seed-Starting Dates   Spring   /   Fall   /

Varieties

....

....

Sources

....

....

Date	Notes on Seed Starting, Cultivation, Harvest, Yield, and Flavor
....	
....	
....	
....	
....	
....	
....	
....	
....	
....	
....	
....	
....	
....	
....	
....	
....	
....	
....	

Crop: .... Year/s

Ideal Seed-Starting Dates   Spring   /   Fall   /

Varieties

....

....

Sources

....

....

Date	Notes on Seed Starting, Cultivation, Harvest, Yield, and Flavor

Crop: ....

Year/s

Ideal Seed-Starting Dates   Spring   /   Fall   /

Varieties

....

....

Sources

....

....

Date	Notes on Seed Starting, Cultivation, Harvest, Yield, and Flavor

Crop: ....

Year/s [   ]

Ideal Seed-Starting Dates [Spring   /   ] [Fall   /   ]

Varieties

....

....

Sources

....

....

Date	Notes on Seed Starting, Cultivation, Harvest, Yield, and Flavor

Crop: ....

Year/s

Ideal Seed-Starting Dates Spring   /   Fall   /

Varieties

....

....

Sources

....

....

Date	Notes on Seed Starting, Cultivation, Harvest, Yield, and Flavor

Crop: .... Year/s [   ]

Ideal Seed-Starting Dates   Spring   / | Fall   /

Varieties

....

....

Sources

....

....

Date	Notes on Seed Starting, Cultivation, Harvest, Yield, and Flavor

Crop: .... Year/s

Ideal Seed-Starting Dates Spring   /   Fall   /

Varieties

....

....

Sources

....

....

Date	Notes on Seed Starting, Cultivation, Harvest, Yield, and Flavor

Crop: .... Year/s [   ]

Ideal Seed-Starting Dates | Spring   / | Fall   /

Varieties

....

....

Sources

....

....

Date	Notes on Seed Starting, Cultivation, Harvest, Yield, and Flavor

Crop: .... Year/s [   ]

Ideal Seed-Starting Dates   Spring   /   Fall   /

Varieties

....

....

Sources

....

....

Date	Notes on Seed Starting, Cultivation, Harvest, Yield, and Flavor

Crop: ....

Year/s [   ]

Ideal Seed-Starting Dates [Spring   /   ] [Fall   /   ]

Varieties

....

....

Sources

....

....

Date	Notes on Seed Starting, Cultivation, Harvest, Yield, and Flavor

Crop: ....

Year/s [   ]

Ideal Seed-Starting Dates [Spring   /   ] [Fall   /   ]

Varieties

....

....

Sources

....

....

Date	Notes on Seed Starting, Cultivation, Harvest, Yield, and Flavor

Crop:

Year/s

Ideal Seed-Starting Dates Spring / Fall /

Varieties

Sources

Date	Notes on Seed Starting, Cultivation, Harvest, Yield, and Flavor

Crop: .... Year/s [   ]

Ideal Seed-Starting Dates   Spring   /   Fall   /

Varieties

....

....

Sources

....

....

Date	Notes on Seed Starting, Cultivation, Harvest, Yield, and Flavor

Crop: .... Year/s [   ]

Ideal Seed-Starting Dates [Spring   /   ] [Fall   /   ]

Varieties

....

....

Sources

....

....

Date	Notes on Seed Starting, Cultivation, Harvest, Yield, and Flavor

Crop: ....

Year/s [ ]

Ideal Seed-Starting Dates   Spring   /   Fall   /

Varieties

....

....

Sources

....

....

Date	Notes on Seed Starting, Cultivation, Harvest, Yield, and Flavor

Crop: ....

Year/s

Ideal Seed-Starting Dates

Spring   /

Fall   /

Varieties

....

....

Sources

....

....

Date	Notes on Seed Starting, Cultivation, Harvest, Yield, and Flavor

Crop: ....

Year/s [   ]

Ideal Seed-Starting Dates Spring   /   Fall   /

Varieties

....

....

Sources

....

....

Date	Notes on Seed Starting, Cultivation, Harvest, Yield, and Flavor

Crop: ....   Year/s

Ideal Seed-Starting Dates   Spring   /   Fall   /

Varieties

....

....

Sources

....

....

Date	Notes on Seed Starting, Cultivation, Harvest, Yield, and Flavor

Crop: .... Year/s [   ]

Ideal Seed-Starting Dates Spring [/   ] Fall [/   ]

Varieties

....

....

Sources

....

....

Date	Notes on Seed Starting, Cultivation, Harvest, Yield, and Flavor

Crop: ....

Ideal Seed-Starting Dates   Spring   /   Fall   /

Varieties

....

....

Sources

....

....

Date	Notes on Seed Starting, Cultivation, Harvest, Yield, and Flavor

Crop: .... Year/s [   ]

Ideal Seed-Starting Dates   Spring [/   ]   Fall [/   ]

Varieties

....

....

Sources

....

....

Date	Notes on Seed Starting, Cultivation, Harvest, Yield, and Flavor

Crop: .... Year/s [   ]

Ideal Seed-Starting Dates   Spring   /   [   ]   Fall   /   [   ]

Varieties

....

....

Sources

....

....

Date	Notes on Seed Starting, Cultivation, Harvest, Yield, and Flavor

Crop: .... Year/s [   ]

Ideal Seed-Starting Dates   Spring   /   Fall   /

Varieties

....

....

Sources

....

....

Date	Notes on Seed Starting, Cultivation, Harvest, Yield, and Flavor

Crop: ....

Year/s

Ideal Seed-Starting Dates   Spring   /   Fall   /

Varieties

....

....

Sources

....

....

Date	Notes on Seed Starting, Cultivation, Harvest, Yield, and Flavor

Crop: .... Year/s [   ]

Ideal Seed-Starting Dates   Spring [/   ]   Fall [/   ]

Varieties

....

....

Sources

....

....

Date	Notes on Seed Starting, Cultivation, Harvest, Yield, and Flavor

Crop:

Ideal Seed-Starting Dates   Spring   /   Fall   /

Varieties

....

....

Sources

....

....

Date	Notes on Seed Starting, Cultivation, Harvest, Yield, and Flavor

Crop: .... Year/s [   ]

Ideal Seed-Starting Dates   Spring   /   [   ]   Fall   /   [   ]

Varieties

....

....

Sources

....

....

Date	Notes on Seed Starting, Cultivation, Harvest, Yield, and Flavor
....	
....	
....	
....	
....	
....	
....	
....	
....	
....	
....	
....	
....	
....	
....	
....	

Crop: ....

Ideal Seed-Starting Dates   Spring   /   Fall   /

Varieties

....

....

Sources

....

....

Date	Notes on Seed Starting, Cultivation, Harvest, Yield, and Flavor

Crop: .... Year/s [   ]

Ideal Seed-Starting Dates Spring [/   ]   Fall [/   ]

Varieties

....

....

Sources

....

....

Date	Notes on Seed Starting, Cultivation, Harvest, Yield, and Flavor

Crop: .... Year/s [   ]

Ideal Seed-Starting Dates   Spring [/   ]   Fall [/   ]

Varieties

....

....

Sources

....

....

Date	Notes on Seed Starting, Cultivation, Harvest, Yield, and Flavor

Crop: ....

Year/s

Ideal Seed-Starting Dates

Spring   /

Fall   /

Varieties

....

....

Sources

....

....

Date	Notes on Seed Starting, Cultivation, Harvest, Yield, and Flavor

Crop: .... Year/s [   ]

Ideal Seed-Starting Dates   Spring   /   Fall   /

Varieties

....

....

Sources

....

....

Date	Notes on Seed Starting, Cultivation, Harvest, Yield, and Flavor

Crop: .... Year/s

Ideal Seed-Starting Dates Spring /   Fall   /

Varieties

....

....

Sources

....

....

Date	Notes on Seed Starting, Cultivation, Harvest, Yield, and Flavor

Crop: .... Year/s [   ]

Ideal Seed-Starting Dates   Spring   /   Fall   /

Varieties

....

....

Sources

....

....

Date	Notes on Seed Starting, Cultivation, Harvest, Yield, and Flavor

Crop: .... Year/s [   ]

Ideal Seed-Starting Dates Spring [/   ] Fall [/   ]

Varieties

....

....

Sources

....

....

Date	Notes on Seed Starting, Cultivation, Harvest, Yield, and Flavor

Crop: .... Year/s [   ]

Ideal Seed-Starting Dates   Spring   /   Fall   /

Varieties

....

....

Sources

....

....

Date	Notes on Seed Starting, Cultivation, Harvest, Yield, and Flavor

Crop: .... Year/s

Ideal Seed-Starting Dates   Spring   /   Fall   /

Varieties

....

....

Sources

....

....

Date	Notes on Seed Starting, Cultivation, Harvest, Yield, and Flavor

Crop: .... Year/s [   ]

Ideal Seed-Starting Dates   Spring   /   Fall   /

Varieties
....
....

Sources
....
....

Date	Notes on Seed Starting, Cultivation, Harvest, Yield, and Flavor

Crop: .... Year/s [   ]

Ideal Seed-Starting Dates | Spring   / | | Fall   / |

Varieties

....

....

Sources

....

....

Date	Notes on Seed Starting, Cultivation, Harvest, Yield, and Flavor

Crop: ....

Year/s

Ideal Seed-Starting Dates

Spring   /

Fall   /

Varieties

....

....

Sources

....

....

Date	Notes on Seed Starting, Cultivation, Harvest, Yield, and Flavor

Crop:

Ideal Seed-Starting Dates   Spring   /   Fall   /

Varieties

....

....

Sources

....

....

Date	Notes on Seed Starting, Cultivation, Harvest, Yield, and Flavor

Crop: .... Year/s [   ]

Ideal Seed-Starting Dates [Spring   /   ] [Fall   /   ]

Varieties

....

....

Sources

....

....

Date	Notes on Seed Starting, Cultivation, Harvest, Yield, and Flavor

Crop: .... Year/s [   ]

Ideal Seed-Starting Dates   Spring   /   Fall   /

Varieties

....

....

Sources

....

....

Date	Notes on Seed Starting, Cultivation, Harvest, Yield, and Flavor

Crop:

Year/s

Ideal Seed-Starting Dates   Spring   /   Fall   /

Varieties

Sources

Date	Notes on Seed Starting, Cultivation, Harvest, Yield, and Flavor

Crop: .... Year/s

Ideal Seed-Starting Dates | Spring / | Fall /

Varieties

....

....

Sources

....

....

Date	Notes on Seed Starting, Cultivation, Harvest, Yield, and Flavor

Crop: .... Year/s [ ]

Ideal Seed-Starting Dates Spring [/   ] Fall [/   ]

Varieties

....

....

Sources

....

....

Date	Notes on Seed Starting, Cultivation, Harvest, Yield, and Flavor

Crop: .... Year/s

Ideal Seed-Starting Dates   Spring   /   Fall   /

Varieties

....

....

Sources

....

....

Date	Notes on Seed Starting, Cultivation, Harvest, Yield, and Flavor
....	
....	
....	
....	
....	
....	
....	
....	
....	
....	
....	
....	
....	
....	
....	
....	
....	
....	

Crop: .... Year/s [   ]

Ideal Seed-Starting Dates   Spring   [/]   Fall   [/]

Varieties

....

....

Sources

....

....

Date	Notes on Seed Starting, Cultivation, Harvest, Yield, and Flavor

Crop: .... Year/s

Ideal Seed-Starting Dates | Spring   / | Fall   /

Varieties

....

....

Sources

....

....

Date	Notes on Seed Starting, Cultivation, Harvest, Yield, and Flavor
......	
......	
......	
......	
......	
......	
......	
......	
......	
......	
......	
......	
......	
......	
......	
......	
......	

Crop: ....

Year/s

Ideal Seed-Starting Dates

Spring   /

Fall   /

Varieties

....

....

Sources

....

....

Date	Notes on Seed Starting, Cultivation, Harvest, Yield, and Flavor

Crop:

Year/s

Ideal Seed-Starting Dates Spring / Fall /

Varieties

....

....

Sources

....

....

Date	Notes on Seed Starting, Cultivation, Harvest, Yield, and Flavor

Crop: .... Year/s [   ]

Ideal Seed-Starting Dates   Spring   /   Fall   /

Varieties

....

....

Sources

....

....

Date	Notes on Seed Starting, Cultivation, Harvest, Yield, and Flavor

Crop: .... Year/s [   ]

Ideal Seed-Starting Dates   Spring   /   Fall   /

Varieties

....

....

Sources

....

....

Date	Notes on Seed Starting, Cultivation, Harvest, Yield, and Flavor

Crop: ....

Ideal Seed-Starting Dates   Spring   /   Fall   /

Varieties
....

....

Sources
....

....

Date	Notes on Seed Starting, Cultivation, Harvest, Yield, and Flavor

Crop: .... Year/s [ ]

Ideal Seed-Starting Dates   Spring   /   Fall   /

Varieties

....

....

Sources

....

....

Date	Notes on Seed Starting, Cultivation, Harvest, Yield, and Flavor
....	
....	
....	
....	
....	
....	
....	
....	
....	
....	
....	
....	
....	
....	
....	
....	
....	
....	
....	

Crop: .... Year/s [   ]

Ideal Seed-Starting Dates [Spring   /   ] [Fall   /   ]

Varieties

....

....

Sources

....

....

Date	Notes on Seed Starting, Cultivation, Harvest, Yield, and Flavor

Crop: .... Year/s [   ]

Ideal Seed-Starting Dates Spring /   Fall /

Varieties

....

....

Sources

....

....

Date	Notes on Seed Starting, Cultivation, Harvest, Yield, and Flavor

Illustration Credits

Cover illustrations by Bailey, L. H., *Garden-Making* (New York: The Macmillan Company, 1898) 356, front (t.c.); Bailey, L. H., *Garden-Making* (New York: The Macmillan Company, 1898) 360, front (m.c.r.); Bailey, L. H., *Garden-Making* (New York: The Macmillan Company, 1898) 379, back (2nd f.t.c.r.); Bailey, L. H., *Standard Cyclopedia of Horticulture* (New York: The Macmillan Company, 1917), back (2nd f.t. & l., 3rd f.t.c., 2nd f.t.l., m.c.), front (2nd f.b.l. [flower], 2nd f.t.r., 3rd f.t.c.l., 5th f.t.r., b.c.l., b.l., m.c.l., t. 2nd f.l., t.l., 2nd f.l. & 3rd f.t.); Beard, Frank, *Bible Symbols or The Bible in Pictures* (Chicago: Hertel, Jenkins, and Co., 1904) 38, back (2nd f.t.c.l.), front (2nd f.b.r.); Chambers, William & Robert, *Encyclopaedia—A Dictionary of Universal Knowledge for the People* (Philadelphia: J. B. Lippincott & Co., 1881), back (2nd f.b.r. [large leaves and flowers], b.c.l.), front (2nd f.b.l., large leaves and flowers); *Chambers's Encyclopedia* (Philadelphia: J. B. Lippincott Company, 1875), IFC; Extrait du livre *Fleurs plantes et fruits*, 1903/public domain/Wikimedia Commons, back (t.r.); Flint, Charles L., *Grasses and Forage Plants* (Boston: William F. Gill & Company, 1874), back (b.l.); Gager, C. Stuart, *Fundamentals of Botany* (Philadelphia, PA: P. Blakiston), front (b.c.); courtesy of Grovida Gardening, www.grovida.us/CC BY 3.0, back (2nd f.b.l.), front (3rd f.b.l.); Hall, Guillermo, *Poco a Poco: An Elementary Direct Method for Learning Spanish* (Hudson, NY: World Book Company, 1922), back (2nd f.t.r. and 2nd f.b.r. [watermelons]), front (2nd f.b.l., watermelons); Holst, B. P., *The Teachers' and Pupils' Cyclopaedia* (Kansas City: The Bufton Book Company, 1909), back (m.l.), front (3rd f.l.c.); Kantner, *Book of Objects* 144, back (2nd f.b.r., two melons in front), front (2nd f.b.l., two melons in front); Kennerly, C. H., *Facts and Figures or The A B C of Florida Trucking* (St. Augustine: The Record Company, 1911) 55, front (3rd f.b. & 2nd f.r.); Kennerly, C. H., *Facts and Figures or The A B C of Florida Trucking* (St. Augustine: The Record Company, 1911) 98, back (3rd f.b.c.l., b.r.); Kennerly, C. H., *Facts and Figures or The A B C of Florida Trucking* (St. Augustine: The Record Company, 1911) 102, front (2nd f.b. & 2nd f.r.); © Morphart/Depositphotos.com, front (3rd f.t.r.); Nicholson, George, *The Illustrated Dictionary of Gardening*, Div. VI (London: L. Upcott Gill, 1884), back (2nd f.b.c., 2nd f.t. & r., m.c.r., t.c.l., t.c.r.), front (b.r., 2nd f.b. & l., 3rd f.b.c.l. [leaves], 3rd f.b.r., m.c.), IBC; © Patrick Guenette/Dreamstime.com, front (t.r.); © Quagga Media/Alamy Stock Photo, front (2nd f.t. & l.); Rawson, W. W., *Success in Market Gardening: A New Growers' Manual* (Boston: W. W. Rawson, 1892), front (3rd f.b.c.l., beet body); back (2nd f.b.c.l., 2nd f.b.c.r., 3rd f.t.c.l, t.l.), front (2nd f.t.c.r., 2nd f.t.l., 3rd f.b.c.r., 4th f.t.r., t. 2nd f.r., t.c.r.); Schäk, Joseph, *Drittes Lesebuch* (New York: Fr. Pustet, 1874) 158, front (b.c.r.); Vaughan, L. Brent, *Hill's Practical Reference Library of General Knowledge* (New York: Dixon, Hanson & Company, 1906), front (2nd f.b.c.l.), back (3rd f.t.r.); Whitney, William Dwight, *The Century Dictionary: An Encyclopedic Lexicon of the English Language* (New York: The Century Co., 1911), front (2nd f.l.c.)

Interior illustrations by Bailey, L. H., *Garden-Making* (New York: The Macmillan Company, 1898) 356, 66 and throughout; Bailey, L. H., *Garden-Making* (New York: The Macmillan Company, 1898) 360, 62 and throughout; Bailey, L. H., *Garden-Making* (New York: The Macmillan Company, 1898) 379, 84 and throughout; Bailey, L. H., *Standard Cyclopedia of Horticulture* (New York: The Macmillan Company, 1917), 1 (t.l., 2nd f.b. & l., 2nd f.t.r., 4th f.t.r., c., m.c.l.), 6 (t.l., 2nd f.t.r., l.m., m.c., t.c.l.), 7 (t.l.,

m.c.r., 2nd f.t.l.), 16 (2nd f.t.c.l.), 20 (2nd f.b.r., 2nd f.t.l., m.c.l.), 21 (t.c.r.), 38 and throughout, 42 and throughout, 58 (t., vine with flower) and throughout and (b.r.) and throughout, 72 and throughout, 80 (t.) and throughout; Bailey, L. H., *Standard Cyclopedia of Horticulture* (New York: The Macmillan Company, 1917) vol. 4, pg. 2332, 6 (2nd f.t.c.l.); Beard, Frank, *Bible Symbols or The Bible in Pictures* (Chicago: Hertel, Jenkins, and Co., 1904) 38, 6 (t.c.), 20 (t.c.l.); Bercy, Paul, *Simples Notions de Francais* (New York: William R. Jenkins, 1894), 7 (4th f.t.l.), 20 (3rd f.t.c.); Bergen, Joseph Y., A. M. *Elements of Botany* (Boston: Ginn & Company, 1896), 7 (b.c.); Brent, L., *Vaughan Hill's Practical Reference Library of General Knowledge* (New York: Dixon, Hanson & Company, 1906), 6 (t.c.r.), 7 (2nd f.t.r.), 70 and throughout; *Chambers's Encyclopedia* (Philadelphia: J. B. Lippincott Company, 1875), 24 (r.) and throughout; Chambers, William & Robert, *Encyclopaedia—A Dictionary of Universal Knowledge for the People* (Philadelphia: J. B. Lippincott & Co., 1881), 1 (c.m.l.), 6 (2nd f.t.c.), 7 (t.c.l., t.c.), 20 (3rd f.t.l.), 21 (2nd f.b.r.), 58 (t., large leaves and flowers) and throughout; ClipArt ETC, 6 (2nd f.t.l.), 7 (3rd f.b.r.); Extrait du livre, *Fleurs plantes et fruits*, 1903/public domain/Wikimedia Commons, 26 and throughout; Flint, Charles L., *Grasses and Forage Plants* (Boston: William F. Gill & Company, 1874), 44 and throughout; Gager, C. Stuart, *Fundamentals of Botany* (Philadelphia: P. Blakiston), 6 (2nd f.b.r.), 7 (b.l.), 20 (2nd f.t.c.r.), 21 (3rd f.b.c.l., b.r.), 40, 88 (2nd f.b.l.); courtesy of Grovida Gardening, www.grovida.us/CC BY 3.0, 22 and throughout; Hall, Guillermo, *Poco a Poco: An Elementary Direct Method for Learning Spanish* (Hudson, NY: World Book Company, 1922), 7 (2nd f.b.r.), 20 (2nd f.b.c.), 58 (t., watermelons) and throughout; Holst, B. P., *The Teachers' and Pupils' Cyclopaedia* (Kansas City: The Bufton Book Company, 1909), 7 (2nd f.b. & r.), 80 (b.) and throughout; Katner, *Book of Objects* 144, 58 (t., two melons in front) and throughout; Kennerly, C. H., *Facts and Figures or The A B C of Florida Trucking* (St. Augustine: The Record Company, 1911) 55, 56 and throughout; Kennerly, C. H., *Facts and Figures or The A B C of Florida Trucking* (St. Augustine: The Record Company, 1911) 98, 21 (m.c.), 68 and throughout; Kennerly, C. H., *Facts and Figures or The A B C of Florida Trucking* (St. Augustine: The Record Company, 1911) 102, 1 (2nd f.b.r.), 6 (b.l.); © Morphart/Depositphotos.com, 78 and throughout; Nicholson, George, *The Illustrated Dictionary of Gardening*, Div. VI (London: L. Upcott Gill, 1884), 1 (b.r.), 3, 7 (t.c.r., m.c.l., b.r.), 20 (b.r.), 21 (2nd f.t.c.r.), 30 (leaves) and throughout, 32 and throughout, 34, 36, 48 and throughout, 50 and throughout, 54 and throughout, 64, 74 and throughout, 82 and throughout, 89 (t.c.); © Patrick Guenette/Dreamstime.com, 76 and throughout; © Quagga Media/Alamy Stock Photo, 1 (t.c.l.), 6 (m.c.l.); 21 (3rd f.b.l.); Rawson, W. W., *Success in Market Gardening: A New Growers' Manual* (Boston: W. W. Rawson, 1892), 1 (t.c.r., 2nd f.t.r., b.c.), 5, 6 (2nd f.t.c.r., 3rd f.b.r., r.m.), 7 (r.m.), 20 (3rd f.t.c.l., 2nd f.t.r.), 21 (t.l.), 24 (l.) and throughout, 30 (beet body) and throughout, 46 and throughout, 60 and throughout, 86 and throughout; Schäk, Joseph, *Drittes Lesebuch* (New York: Fr. Pustet, 1874) 158, 28 and throughout; Whitney, William Dwight, *The Century Dictionary: An Encyclopedic Lexicon of the English Language* (New York: The Century Co., 1911), 1 (c.m.l), 7 (t.c.), 20 (3rd f.t.l.)

All illustrations are sourced from ClipArt ETC (https://etc.usf.edu/clipart), unless marked otherwise

ABOUT THE CREATOR OF THIS PLANNER

Lynn Byczynski is the author of two books, *Market Farming Success* and *The Flower Farmer: An Organic Grower's Guide to Raising and Selling Cut Flowers*. A longtime market farmer, she founded *Growing for Market* magazine, which she published for 25 years. She currently owns Seeds from Italy, the US distributor for Italy's oldest seed company, Franchi Sementi. Her website is GrowItalian.com.